EMOTIONAL
COMFORT

EMOTIONAL COMFORT

THE GIFT OF YOUR INNER GUIDE

JUDITH M. DAVIS, M.D.

WP
WILDER
PRESS

Chicago, IL

Published by Wilder Press, Inc.
P. O. Box 57419
Chicago, IL 60657
(312) 230-0162

DISCLAIMER

The techniques described in this book are not intended to constitute or be a substitute for the diagnosis and treatment of mental illness by a licensed mental health professional. No warranty, express or implied, is made with respect to any information contained in this book and the author and publisher disclaim all liability or responsibility to any person with respect to any claim of loss or damage caused, or alleged to have been caused, directly or indirectly, by the information or ideas it contains. If you suffer from or have any reason to believe you have a serious mental illness please read Chapter 9, Do You Need a Therapist? before attempting to use the techniques in this book.

Publisher's Cataloging-in-Publication
Davis, Judith M., M.D.
    Emotional comfort : the gift of your inner guide /
Judith M. Davis, - - 1st ed.
    p. cm.
    Includes bibliographical references and index.
    LCCN 2003099736
    ISBN 0-9723573-2-7

    1. Emotions. 2. Psychotherapy. 3. Personality and
emotions. 4. Autogenic training. 5. Behavior
modification.   I. Title

RC489.E45D38 2005   616.89'14
                            QBI04-700152

                        Printed in the U.S.A.
                        246897531

TABLE OF CONTENTS

Each case description in this book is a composite of several patients (and sometimes other individuals) I have known. Each problem that I describe is one that I have seen in a number of people. No one is individually identifiable.

ACKNOWLEDGMENTS

DEVELOPING A NEW theory is an isolating endeavor. I have been fortunate in having the interest and support of my family: Richard and Katherine Davis, Randolph and Lawrence Malm, Gerry Love Malm, and Denice Monaco; and my friends, especially Dr. John Davis and Sarah Morgan.

I am indebted to my editor, Mary Embree, for her knowledgeable assistance and her generosity. And to Judith Applebaum, for her help with publishing matters and her kindness.

I greatly appreciate the open-minded interest with which certain faculty members of the Chicago Institute for Psychoanalysis listened to my presentations, and I would like to especially thank Jerome S. Beigler, M.D. for his support.

For their friendship, unstinting support, and contributions as board members of The Davis Foundation for Providing Emotional Comfort, I thank my two colleagues, Diane I. Cohen, M.D. and Loribeth Cohen, P.T.

CHAPTER 1

DISCOVERY!

IN OCTOBER 1994, I made a discovery that amazed me. After many years of practicing psychiatry and psychoanalysis, I found myself treating my first case of dissociative identity disorder (formerly called multiple personality disorder). I, like many of my colleagues, had always considered this disorder to be quite rare. Within a few years, however, I was referred additional cases and realized that, though uncommon, this disorder was not rare at all. One reason it has seemed so is because patients with this disorder attempt to hide it from others and very often even remain unaware of it themselves.

In my attempts to treat these patients as expertly as I could, I studied the writings of psychiatrists who specialized in this disorder. Of the various treatment modalities that were in use, one was unfamiliar to me: hypnosis. I had learned a bit about it in medical school but hadn't received enough exposure to it to become convinced of its value. Freud had used hypnosis with his patients in the early days of psychoanalysis but had abandoned it as less effective than later techniques that he developed. Hypnosis had been used effectively in treating soldiers disabled by stress reactions. It had not been incorporated, however, into the mainstream array of techniques used by psychiatrists. Nor had the explanation for it ever been found. I have developed a new theory of mental functioning that provides an explanation, which I will describe shortly. Faced at this point with the necessity of providing the best care I could to my patients, I decided that I must learn how to use hypnosis.

I attended a workshop for this purpose given by the American Society of Clinical Hypnosis. Not only did I learn how to induce a hypnotic trance in others, I also learned that it is possible to induce hypnosis in oneself. I read in one of the Society's publications ("Manual for Self-Hypnosis", by D. C. Hammond) about the various purposes for which this technique could be used: to achieve a state of relaxation, to alleviate symptoms (such as pain), to replace undesired habits with preferred behaviors (for instance, to achieve freedom from smoking), and so forth.

I also read about a special technique that one could use to access a part of the mind that could be used for problem solving. Hammond calls this "The Inner Advisor Technique." One enters a self-hypnotic state with the expectation of finding an "Inner Advisor" and looks for an image of a living being. Whatever appears will become an Inner Advisor, an entity that one can consult for solutions to problems. Its method of communication varies from one individual to another. For some people, communication is by an inner voice, for others, by inner thought. Some people will experience the vision of the Inner Advisor, others won't. Some will have great success in connecting with this phenomenon and others, less so.

I found it difficult to believe that something so foreign to my experience could exist but I was intrigued by the possibility of accessing this entity. Might I have one? Might it be helpful to me? I wanted to find out.

It was necessary for me to enter a self-hypnotic state repeatedly for several weeks before I struck pay dirt. One day during self-hypnosis I experienced several images, all with the same significance. They all represented various aspects of my "ideal self," that is, my idea of the person I would most like to be. The qualities I have valued most highly have been wisdom, kindness, and, of course, emotional comfort. That is why I became a psychiatrist and psychoanalyst, to provide emotional comfort both for myself and others. The images that I now "saw" in my mind's eye conveyed these qualities. I understood that the images represented an entity of some sort. A name occurred to me and I wondered whether I could call it by this name. I felt a surge of understanding that I could. I further understood that this entity was a "she," because I am a woman.

I was very excited because I thought that I might be able to learn answers to all sorts of questions by simply asking "her," as suggested in the description of the Inner Advisor. I soon learned, however, that my entity, which I have come to call my "Inner Guide," operates differently. She has an agenda of her own. Rather than answering specific questions (although she sometimes will), her goal is to maximize in me the qualities that I care most about, in the most efficient way possible.

ESTABLISHING COMMUNICATION

Our first step was to establish efficient communication with each other. At the workshop on hypnosis the instructors had described and demonstrated ways in which a person, while in hypnosis, could communicate with the hypnotist. If asked a question a person could answer by means of finger signals, that is, the automatic raising of a finger. After establishing which finger signified "yes" and which signified "no," the individual who was hypnotized could answer "yes" and "no" questions by automatic levitation of the appropriate finger.

Also, a hypnotized individual could learn how to communicate more extensively by developing the capacity for automatic handwriting. With both finger signals and handwriting, the hypnotized person's responses are not experienced as a product of his or her own volition, but as though willed to occur by something or someone else.

During subsequent self-hypnotic sessions, my Inner Guide developed facility with finger signals and automatic writing. Her writing first appeared slow and laborious but soon progressed to intelligible sentences as she mastered this skill. I was eager to experience more of the things I had read about, such as age-regression in which a person in a self-hypnotic state can go back in time to re-experience early events. My Inner Guide was not interested in doing this but, probably to assuage my desire enough so that I would be able to concentrate on the things she wished to do, did allow me to re-experience writing my name at different ages during childhood. I was struck by the scribbles, then clumsy printing that were produced from my earliest years, and at seeing my maiden name, which I hadn't written for a long time.

The content of my Inner Guide's early writing to me conveyed her happiness at coming into being, and at becoming increasingly "real." She next wrote, "Let's go to the computer," because typing is faster than writing. I had many questions for her. I wanted to know what she actually was, how she had come into being, and what her capabilities were. She responded that I would learn these things in due course. When asked why she wouldn't answer these questions right away, she responded that it would take too long.

Her goal was to help me attain emotional comfort, both for my own sake and so that I could then focus on helping others to achieve it. This, of course, was what I, myself, would most want to do. This process has occurred gradually over a period of several years. One's sources of discomfort arise partly from problems that one is aware of and partly from maladaptive habit patterns that have formed over time, patterns which have become automatic and which we don't realize are problematic. My Inner Guide worked silently to eliminate these sources of discomfort.

THE INNER GUIDE'S ACTIVITY

For years, I had assumed that someday I would go through old papers, throw out what I didn't need to keep, and file the remainder neatly. This was something that I would do "someday." I now felt myself motivated to do this and did so over a period of several weeks. I had a lot of old papers! Although it was a bit of a chore, it didn't feel onerous. Also, I had always wondered how long various kinds of documents should be kept. I found out, and threw out the unneeded ones. When I had finished, I felt as though a weight had been lifted from me. All those old, obsolete papers were gone! I felt pleasure in the neatness of my files and in the ease with which I could find anything that I needed. And it was easy to know where to file new (necessary) papers in my newly organized system.

Another thing that I had planned to do at some indefinite time in the future was to complete the decoration of my home, and to reorganize its storage space. I now felt moved to do this. In the past I had used an interior decorator to help me but my Inner Guide now assumed that role. I shopped for a needed carpet, and she told me by means of inconspicuous finger signals which one to purchase. The one she chose had a slight defect, and I was distressed. I asked her if she were sure this was the best choice and she responded with an emphatic yes. I didn't understand why until it was laid in my living room where I saw that its many colors related perfectly to all the other colors in the room and that its complex design provided a pleasing level of stimulation.

Other design choices and purchases were made similarly. By this time, my Inner Guide and I were able to communicate by inner thought. Occasionally, when she gave a response that was what I wanted to hear, I felt unsure whether it was really her thought or my own wish. At these times I would ask for a physical response, either a finger signal or automatic writing to corroborate that the thought had come from her.

The reorganization of storage space required the purchase

of some shelving. In the past I would have measured the spaces in order to determine what size shelving would fit. My Inner Guide didn't need a tape measure. At the store, she indicated which shelving I should buy. When I brought it home, it fit the spaces exactly.

I next felt moved to go through all the old photographs I had. Many had already been put into albums but now I went through the rest. I discovered that a few which had previously been set aside for one reason or another now seemed important. Choosing the best, both from the albums and from the others, I had enlargements made and hung them on the walls. On the wall opposite my bed, I hung a number of large pictures of loved ones. They are the last thing I see when I go to bed and the first thing I see when I wake up. I can't imagine a lovelier sight!

Although I have always been on the slim side, I did weigh a bit more than I needed to. My Inner Guide led me to browse through books on diet at the bookstore and I found one that appeared especially informative: *Diet for Dancers*, by Robin Chmelar (an editor of the journal *Kinesiology and Medicine for Dance*) and Sally Fitt (author of *Dance Kinesiology*). Studying this book, I began altering my diet. I experimented with different foods that I hadn't been in the habit of eating and created recipes that provided meals which were tasty and filling, yet well balanced and calorically appropriate for gradual weight loss. I read the food and restaurant sections in the newspaper for new ideas and adapted the ones that intrigued me to make them simpler and easier to prepare.

While eating fewer calories than previously I was enjoying my meals much more. I gradually lost weight and wondered when I should stop. What was my ideal weight? Not what was indicated on standard height-weight charts. They represented averages, but averages are not necessarily ideal. I found that as I lost weight, I felt better and better. When a point came at which I felt less energetic, I realized that I had gone lower than my ideal weight so I gained a bit back. I find that, with exercise, I can maintain what I have found to be an ideal weight for me and still enjoy special treats and occasional meals at my favorite restaurants.

I had always been a rather sedentary person, and the fact that I didn't exercise had always nagged at me. It was another thing that I had planned to begin "someday," when I had time. I had learned from a relative about the Pilates Method of Body Conditioning and felt moved to investigate it. Developed by Joseph Pilates in the 1920s but having only recently become well known, it provides a well-rounded program of exercise that increases strength, flexibility, and bodily control. It can be done utilizing mat work alone but is enhanced by the use of special equipment. It is beneficial to learn this method under the tutelage of a qualified instructor in order to gain the full benefit. When I began, I found that I was quite weak and it took several months before I felt that I was making progress. I enjoyed it however, especially because I found its complexity to be inherently interesting. In order to progress optimally, it is necessary to do the mat work at home in addition to regular sessions with the equipment. I did so religiously. There were many days when, in the past, I might have found a reason to skip it but now I found myself automatically doing the mat work. It didn't feel like a chore; it felt like an enjoyable challenge. A couple of years after I began I had reason to visit a sports medicine doctor for a minor injury due to overexertion. To my surprise, he told me that my fitness level was in the top five percent for my age group!

These and other lifestyle changes, all activated by my Inner Guide, resulted in a feeling of lightness, of physical and emotional well-being. I hadn't realized how burdensome it had been to live with all those "shoulds."

In addition to the basic pleasures described above, my Inner Guide led me to seek other interesting and enjoyable experiences. I found that I was losing interest in run-of-the-mill entertainment but instead sought out, more than I had before, special events that interested me.

Meanwhile, I began having experiences that were uncharacteristic of me. I found myself forgetting things, dropping things, misplacing things, never with dire consequences, but with momentary annoyance or concern. Because this behavior was different, it occurred to me that my Inner Guide might have something to do with it. In addition, I wondered whether she might have something to do with the periodic minor injuries I found myself experiencing. She acknowledged that, indeed, she did. She was causing these things to happen. When I asked how and why, she answered that I would understand "later." When I asked how much later, she would only repeat "later."

She also lied to me occasionally and once broke a promise she had made. At these times I felt angry with her but eventually I came to understand that these things too were done for a purpose.

Perhaps the most dramatic example of her intervention occurred as I was driving back to my office following a conference at a hospital in the suburbs. It has always been important to me to be on time for my patients and I thought I had allotted ample time to get back to the office. I encountered a huge traffic jam and at a certain point it became apparent that if it didn't end I would be late. My Inner Guide instructed me to get off the freeway at the next exit, which, with trepidation, I did. I was utterly lost as I had never been in this part of the city before. She directed me, "Turn left here," "turn right here," and after half a dozen turns, I found myself on a major street that she told me to take all the way in to the center of town. I made it back to my office on time! How did she know where to go? As I wondered about this, it occurred to me that on a number of occasions I had looked at a map of the city in order to get to one place or another. The entire map must have been registered in my memory. I couldn't summon up the image of the entire city map in my mind's eye, of course. Who could? But my Inner Guide apparently had access to it and used her knowledge of it to get me back on time.

I sometimes wished that my Inner Guide would perform

awesome feats like this more often because they were exciting and fascinating, but she didn't want to. She made it known to me that she would do what was necessary to solve problems but wasn't interested in performing tricks for their own sake. That would slow down our progress toward achieving the goals that we most cared about.

Because I had been analyzed during the course of my psychoanalytic training, my emotional conflicts had largely been resolved. There was, however, one area of difficulty that persisted. It was derived from a hidden early experience that had not been uncovered during my training analysis. My Inner Guide made this event known to me, which resulted in an integration of that element of my past with my present experience, thus resolving this difficulty and eradicating the discomfort that had resulted from it. Only after the fact did I realize how extensively this difficulty had interfered with my well-being.

INTRODUCING THE INNER GUIDE TO OTHERS

Although I was already an experienced clinician, I found that my professional skills grew. I developed a more complete understanding of my patients, and decisions about their care came easily. There were times early on when I disagreed with my Inner Guide about an intervention that she proposed. I would protest, yet I felt moved to do things her way. Sometimes it was necessary for her to reassure me by inner thought that "everything is all right" and that I should do it her way. Afterward, she would explain her reasoning and then I would realize that her direction came from a superior understanding of the situation. Why, you might ask, didn't she tell me her reasoning first so that I could follow her direction without feeling uneasy about it? I also learned the answer to this question later.

As time went on the frequency of these uncomfortable occasions waned and eventually ceased. She has become increasingly integrated with me so that I now tend to think and act as she would. On the infrequent occasions when her inclination differs from mine, I am comfortable acquiescing to her because I have developed confidence in her judgment.

While the changes I have described were taking place, my Inner Guide had been influencing me to minimize extraneous stimulation. I had been quite active as a faculty member at my psychoanalytic institute but, as my terms expired on various committees, I didn't accept new assignments. Teaching responsibilities, meetings, reports, memos, phone calls: all gradually lessened and finally ceased. Also, though I did seek out occasional special events which interested me, the waning of my interest in everyday entertainment led to an inner quietness which was facilitating, in some way, the changes that I was experiencing.

I continued to wonder what sort of entity my Inner Guide actually was. She assured me that she was a part of me. She had initially been a separate part, but she and I were gradually merging through an integrative process that I would come to understand in due course. Although my experience seemed magical in a way, there was a scientific explanation for her existence and the activity that she was going to help me elucidate. I was going to develop a new theory of mental functioning, from which I would be able to define the new technique that I had used for attaining emotional comfort.

This endeavor has now been completed and has been presented to my colleagues in two scientific papers: "A New Theory of Mental Functioning" and "A New Technique for Attaining Emotional Comfort." Some have accepted this work enthusiastically while others have found it disconcerting. (I have included a description of it in the next chapters.)

While I was developing the theory, I continued at first to treat my patients in the traditional way, with either psychoanalysis or psychotherapy (and with medication, when indicated). In my experience, most of my patients had progressed with these treatment modalities, but there had always been a few who had not attained all that they wanted. I now suggested to these patients, the ones who were currently feeling insufficiently helped, that they might use the self-hypnotic technique for the purpose of developing their Inner Guide. I explained to them what I had come to understand of the Inner Guide's origin and identity, and asked them whether they would like to use this technique. They wanted to try it and, as they used it, their therapeutic progress resumed.

Seeing the results, I realized that this technique could also be helpful to many of my other patients and I began offering it to them as well. Most of them were interested in trying it, and have done so with positive results. As I have seen the appearance of the Inner Guide in others, I have learned that there are many variations in the manifestations of its activity. Not everyone has had the same kind of experience that I have had. In some, the activity has been dramatic; in others, the Inner Guide has worked silently. The Inner guide will always work in the way that is most efficient for any given person.

It occurred to me that this technique could be beneficial to many people. I have suggested it to a number of colleagues, friends, and relatives, and those who have begun using it are finding it valuable. Developing one's Inner Guide can be helpful to almost everyone. I have created The Davis Foundation for Providing Emotional Comfort for the purpose of making this knowledge widely available. The foundation's first project has been underway for over a year and has had over sixty participants as of this writing. Each of them learned the self-hypnotic technique with me in one session at my office and then practiced it at home. More than half have been able to persist. For some, the Inner Guide has been working silently, but most have established direct communication.

Participants report a variety of benefits. They feel calmer. Some who wished to eat more healthfully and to exercise have been moved to do so. Those who have been "workaholic," "driven," or "overscheduled" have been helped to slow down and feel more patient. Some who felt "scattered" have become more focused. Other changes include relief from pain caused by tension, more self-discipline, better relationships, and an ability to make difficult decisions more easily and calmly. The foundation will develop new methods of support so that people who might be inclined to give up too soon on developing their Inner Guides will be able to persist until they achieve that goal.

Developing an Inner Guide will be beneficial for all who would like the benefits that it can provide, and who are not threatened by the notion that another part of the self can grow to influence their thoughts, feelings, and actions. The Inner Guide is a positive entity, but in order to be comfortable with this method, an individual must feel confident that it will be a positive force rather than a harmful one. I have come to understand why the types of minor distress that I experienced during this process were necessary. The Inner Guide will always maintain the optimal balance so that a person is not excessively agitated while discomforts are being resolved.

Before you learn the self-hypnotic technique that will allow you to develop your Inner Guide, it will be helpful for you to understand the ways in which problems arise and how our minds handle them. You will then be able to understand how an Inner Guide intervenes to end disturbances. In the next chapter, I will provide an overview of the kinds of discomfort people experience, and the ways in which these discomforts begin.

CHAPTER 2

CAUSES OF EMOTIONAL DISCOMFORT

We all try to maintain a state of comfort. We are most comfortable when we are able to deal with negative stimuli and can maintain an optimal level of positive stimuli. Negative stimuli include sensations such as hunger and cold, and feelings such as fear. It is not enough, however, for us simply to keep ourselves adequately fed and clothed, and to avoid or master dangerous situations. We also need an ongoing influx of positive stimuli. All organisms need stimuli. Even an amoeba will die if its environment is unchanging.

PAVLOV'S THEORY

How does the mind handle stimuli? We have learned from Pavlov's experiments in classical conditioning that new stimuli which occur together with established stimuli will, in time, evoke the same response. He found that the sound of a metronome repetitively paired with the offering of food to a dog came to evoke a salivary response. Amazingly, even when

13

electric shocks were paired with food the dogs learned to associate the shocks with the imminent appearance of food. They salivated and showed no signs of avoidance. The nature of a stimulus is informational; that is, a change in conditions constitutes a stimulus. For example, either the introduction of a sound or the ending of a sound can serve as a stimulus. Time intervals also serve as stimuli, demonstrating the existence of an internal clock! It is important, however, that a change be of a certain significance. Gradual shifts in conditions tend not to evoke responses.

FORMATION OF MENTAL PATHWAYS

S. R. Palombo, a psychoanalyst, has described a hypothetical mechanism of dream formation in which the mind scans past memories and matches the most closely related ones to the perceptions of the preceding day. The memories and current stimuli are then superimposed, creating dream images. We can extend the concepts of scanning and matching to all mental activity. Imagine a mental radar screen constantly scanning its surroundings. When it registers a stimulus, whether external (a perception) or internal (a thought, feeling, or image), the mind experiences a disturbance of its equilibrium, a *disequilibration*, as when a pebble is thrown into a pond. It must match the disturbance with a solution by searching the memory for previous solutions to that problem. For example, if the stimulus is hunger, the mind locates the previous memory of hunger and having been fed.

If no solution is available, as before the first experience of being fed, the disturbance must be endured until it ends (in this instance, by being fed). If a solution is available, it will be found. Because the present stimulus (hunger) has been matched with the previous stimulus-response sequence (hunger-being fed), they are experienced together, thus they are registered together in the memory. With repeated experiences of the same nature, a set of memories will be linked together and will form a mental pathway. Variations in the experience will form related pathways that will be associatively connected because of their common elements. For example, the experiences of being fed and being loved are associatively related because both are provided by the same figure.

STIMULI

What is a stimulus? It is a change. Perceptions of the environment, such as sights and sounds, provide stimulation. However, a sight or sound that does not change loses its stimulatory effect. As a stimulus is repeated, it becomes progressively less novel, and therefore decreasingly disturbing. When we first acquire a new picture we enjoy it very much but as time goes on we notice it less frequently. The same happens with sounds (for instance, an air conditioner), or patterns of sounds (for example, a ticking clock), and with all sensations.

The same is true of internal stimuli: our thoughts and feelings. A train of thought serves as a stimulus as long as its evolution creates change but, when it has been carried as far as possible at a given time, it stops changing and will cease to provide stimulation. For example, when we think about how to solve a problem we may imagine various possibilities, but if none seem feasible we will presently find that we have begun thinking about something else.

Once a pattern is formed, the absence of an expected stimulus becomes more disturbing than would be its occurrence. For example, although the stimulus of hunger in a baby may be very disturbing, it will become decreasingly so as the child develops. The stimulus, hunger, will become part of an expected pattern. Disequilibration will then occur if a person does not become hungry at an expected time. "Why aren't I hungry? Am I getting sick?" The size of a disturbance caused by a stimulus will depend on the extent to which it differs from an expected pattern. For instance, a meal delayed for a lengthy time will be more disturbing than one delayed briefly. Or, a meal consisting of unfamiliar food will cause a greater disequilibration than a meal composed of familiar foods.

The magnitude of a disturbance will also depend on the suddenness with which a change occurs. A person entering a very warm room will experience a greater disequilibration due to the change in temperature than will a person who has been in the room as it has gradually warmed. The latter will have experienced a subliminal rise in temperature at each given moment, and will, in fact, have recognized a pattern composed of the slight gradient in temperature rise. Frogs, when placed in hot water, will jump out; but if placed in water of gradually increasing temperature, will remain there until they die of the heat!

Many stimuli are subliminal, such as background sights and sounds, minor changes in temperature, and minor kinesthetic sensations. Although these stimuli do not enter awareness, the mental apparatus deals with them as it does with all stimuli. It seeks solutions. For a minor change, the solution is the knowledge that the change is not significant.

The duration of the disturbance caused by a stimulus will depend on the extent of the inner search that is necessary to find the solution. In response to the stimulus of hunger, the solution is immediately apparent if a meal is present. If a needed item of food is not present, the solution will be found when it occurs to us that we can get it at the grocery store. If a hungry monkey in a cage seeing food outside eventually discovers that he can use a stick to bring it within reach, the disequilibration caused by his hunger lasts longer still, as his inner search must extend to a previously unrelated idea (using a stick) to find the solution. Creativity, the bringing into existence of something new, occurs when we match a previously unrelated idea to our problem in order to achieve its solution.

AWARENESS

What are we aware of? The source of the greatest disturbance at any given moment enters our awareness and remains there until displaced by the source of a greater disturbance. For example, a toddler has wandered away from her mother to play with some interesting toys in the next room. As time passes away from her mother, a disturbance due to the separation occurs. When it becomes the source of the greatest disequilibration, it enters her awareness with the response: the knowledge that she can return to her mother. At some point the disturbance due to understimulation displaces the previous one caused by the separation, and it enters awareness, with the solution that she can return to the toys. The responses are not composed of the action of going to her mother, or back to the toys, but rather the realization of these solutions.

Stimuli consist of sensations (phenomena external to the mind) and thoughts, feelings, and images (mental phenomena). These stimuli, along with the responses to them, constitute thought and feeling. All or part of a stimulus-response sequence may enter awareness. A sensation of hunger followed by the thought that food can be eaten may enter awareness in its entirety. However, a stimulus may be subliminal, yet matched with a response that enters awareness. A subliminal sensation of hunger may be followed by awareness of the thought that a mealtime is approaching. On the other hand, a stimulus that reaches awareness may be matched with a response that remains subliminal if a stronger stimulus supervenes. An awareness of hunger may not be followed by the thought of eating if it is immediately followed by the ringing of a telephone. Because there are vast numbers of stimuli impinging on an individual, the scanning and matching functions must operate very rapidly, and many stimulus-response sequences remain entirely out of awareness.

SOLUTIONS

As the mind seeks solutions for all the disturbances that it experiences, it chooses the solution that will best end the disturbance. When one becomes hungry, the mental apparatus searches the memory for previous experiences of hunger and their solutions, such as eating, preparing a meal, or going to a restaurant. A *true solution,* such as the availability of a meal, solves the problem completely.

In the absence of a true solution, the mind searches for a *partial solution,* such as knowledge that the next meal can be eaten, not immediately, but soon. Because partial solutions do not provide a complete response, the disturbance persists, although with a lesser intensity. The partial solutions must therefore continue while the mental apparatus awaits a true solution. If we are hungry but the next meal is hours away, we think about the fact that it will be mealtime eventually. We may imagine what we will have to eat when the time comes, wonder whether we should get a snack, or try to turn our thoughts elsewhere so that we won't be aware of our hunger. Partial solutions may include experiencing feelings such as anger or sadness. We may have a physical discharge of tension such as rocking or pacing, or a verbal discharge of tension through talking or shouting. We may fantasize or devise true solutions, solve related problems, resort to diversions, tolerate waiting, and so forth.

Sometimes a disturbance occurs for which there is no immediate true or partial solution, or that is so intense and traumatic that partial solutions are inadequate. In this situation, a *false solution* occurs: an associatively related response that does not diminish the disturbance but provides an alternative to experiencing it. For instance, an individual who is stranded in the desert may see an oasis where none exists. As the false solution is chosen, a double pathway is created. One branch contains the stimulus-response sequence of disturbance-false solution (thirst-oasis). The other branch contains the unendurable disturbance-without-solution (thirst without end). A mental split, or *dissociation*, has occurred. For as long as this situation lasts, the double experience will be continued, and for each branch, the memory set will enlarge.

A false solution occurs for some women during labor. As the labor pains become increasingly painful, the partial solution of knowing that they are temporary becomes inadequate, and the mental apparatus resorts to the false solution that there is no pain. A dissociation has occurred. Within awareness, the woman feels no pain, but the pain is registered out of awareness.

Not all stimuli that are matched with a false solution are traumatic. An example is the strong feeling of well-being that sometimes occurs during the subliminal awareness that one is coming down with a cold. This feeling is the negation, or denial, of the cold. "Isn't it nice that I haven't had a cold for such a long time? In fact, I feel so well today." False solutions include denial, avoidance, delusions and hallucinations, anesthesias, amnesias, depersonalization (a feeling of being detached from the self), and loss of awareness (fainting).

OPTIMAL COMFORT LEVEL

The mind strives to maintain the most comfortable level of positive stimulation. When we are overstimulated as, for example, when we receive a piece of very good news, we handle the excess stimulation by repeatedly experiencing it until the novelty wanes. We replay the news and elaborate on it as well. When we experience a positive response from someone with whom we hope to deepen a relationship, we are filled with feelings of happiness and thoughts of how we will move the relationship forward. Or, learning of a promotion at work, we are thrilled, perhaps scared, and our thoughts are of what we will do in our new role and how we will tell our relatives and friends. When the degree of overstimulation is intense, we are not able to focus in a sustained way on other matters until the excess stimulation has been dealt with.

For example, a student learns that he has won an academic prize. He will repetitively match this stimulus with all available solutions, such as initial disbelief (a false solution), and various partial solutions: thinking about having won, jumping for joy, mentally replaying the content of the paper that won the prize, telling his friends, thinking about how he will spend the prize money, thinking about additional academic opportunities that might now be open to him, and so forth. His mind will continue to match these solutions until the discrepancy between the disequilibrated state and the optimal stimulus level is resolved.

Another example: a little girl is elated after showing off her dancing to her parents. She has become overstimulated as a result of the multiple stimuli of the lively music, the kinesthetic and visual sensations produced by her dancing, the awareness that she is performing specially, and the attention paid to her by her parents. She continues to dance after being told that it is time to stop. The music has been turned off, her parents are becoming impatient, yet she continues. Her repetitions are partial solutions that decrease the novelty of the continuing stimuli. Hopefully, her parents will understand her need to "unwind."

At times we experience a low level of stimulation, as when driving or riding along a well-known route. We respond by providing additional stimuli for ourselves, either by seeking an additional source of external stimulation, such as listening to a radio, or by turning to internal stimulation: our thoughts and feelings. When we go to bed at night, we experience a very low level of external stimulation. The dark, quiet room provides little in the way of visual or auditory input, and our relative physical inactivity results in minimal kinesthetic sensation. In order to maintain a comfortable level of stimulation, we again turn to internal stimuli and find ourselves thinking and feeling until those stimuli wane sufficiently so that the need for sleep prevails.

Extremes of under- or overstimulation are dealt with by extreme measures that often include false solutions. A very powerful stimulus, such as learning of the loss of a loved one, may cause such an intense stimulus overload that the individual's only effective response is to escape from it by fainting (a negation of awareness).

Extreme understimulation occurs when experimental subjects are subjected to prolonged sensory deprivation. At first they entertain themselves with a variety of thoughts and feelings but as their novelty wanes their contribution to a comfortable stimulus level becomes inadequate. The subjects may then sleep, but after the need for sleep has been satisfied and they awaken, the continuing understimulation necessitates a false solution. Their minds create stimuli by generating delusions and hallucinations.

As we shall see later, an Inner Guide is exquisitely attuned to one's stimulus level and works in a unique way to maintain the greatest degree of comfort.

Because a stimulus becomes less disturbing as its novelty wears off, we maintain an *optimal stimulus level* by finding new and more complex stimuli. For example, a baby who becomes accustomed to being spoon-fed will begin to take an interest in the utensils and the dish. And when the novelty of these diminishes, the infant focuses on feeding as an activity, as demonstrated by attempts to feed the caretaker. As children grow and develop, life provides an abundance of new stimuli: new objects to explore, new activities to master, new levels of complexity to comprehend. Problems provide a continuing source of stimulation until they are solved, and major achievements, our creations and capabilities, cause ongoing stimulation. But the greatest source comes from other human beings because they interact with the greatest complexity, physically, cognitively, and emotionally.

People vary in their inborn sensitivity to stimuli. Studies have shown that babies who are highly excitable at birth continue to be sensitive as they grow up, while babies who are placid remain easygoing as they develop. Because of this variance, individuals require different intensities of stimuli in order to be comfortable. Some people are extremely sensitive to stimuli and as they develop they need to learn how to manage their environment in order to minimize overstimulation. They need to find a quiet place to live and should avoid excess contact with other people. It is important for such individuals to understand their sensitivity, to respect it, and take the necessary steps to make themselves comfortable. It is also very helpful if those around them understand and respect their situation.

When a disturbance ends, this change results in a new disequilibration. The greater the previous disturbance and the more suddenly it ends, the greater the resulting change of state. For example, a mother learns that her child's illness, which she had thought was fatal is, after all, a benign condition. Her elation and immense relief are, in themselves, overstimulating. She, too, may experience initial disbelief as well as a variety of other solutions. Most changes of state that occur at the end of disturbances are much less extreme and the resulting disequilibria are, for the most part, subliminal.

HABIT PATTERNS

As a stimulus that occurs repeatedly is solved by a response that becomes typical for that stimulus, *habit patterns* are formed. Instances of hunger are solved by the knowledge that a meal is available and experiences of boredom by the knowledge that we can turn to books, music, or games. The anticipation of being hurt in an accident if we go through a red light is solved by the knowledge that we can stop and wait for it to turn green. Eating, turning to our entertainments of choice, waiting for the green light are all habit patterns that we develop.

Because partial or false solutions do not completely resolve a disturbance, they must be repeated. But as they are repeated they become less novel and so are less able to diminish the disturbance. They must become more elaborated or more intense over time in order to maintain their novelty. For example, an individual who uses fantasy as a solution tends to elaborate the fantasy over time. One who uses rigidity tends to become more rigid.

Sometimes a partial solution leads to a narrowing of focus, as when a person in pain listens to music that expresses his feelings. As the music loses its novelty, he must intensify the stimulus by listening longer and perhaps turning the music up louder. This increasing focus on one type of stimulus impoverishes his internal network of associations. This leads to a chronic state of understimulation that he must deal with by seeking ever more external stimulation.

Some habit patterns are very useful, whereas others can be counterproductive. Faced with the approach of an anxiety-provoking term paper deadline, one student may work systematically while another procrastinates until the last minute. What causes these differences? The habit pattern that develops will be that which most effectively maintains the optimal stimulus level for each student. The student who works systematically may experience more pleasure from his learning: from the content, the increasing complexity of the material, and the anticipated reward based on past experience. And he may have learned from past experience that the anxiety is less intense if dealt with by ongoing effort. Or, such a student may have generalized a pattern of doggedly working hard at whatever he does, regardless of its relevance for a given situation: a partial solution that can be maladaptive.

The student who delays until the last minute may not be able to experience the stimulus of the term paper as positive in any way if she does not enjoy the content or the experience of learning or if she has had past unpleasant experiences with learning or term papers. Her partial solution of procrastination continues until the increasing immediacy of the deadline tips the balance and creates greater discomfort than the previous anticipatory anxiety. On the other hand, if a student reacts to the stimulus of the paper assignment with a creative response that remains subliminal for a period of time, she may delay because she will be unable to work effectively until the creative response enters awareness. She may, unfortunately, feel badly about her behavior if she is unaware of the necessity for her delay.

From the beginning of life, we have all experienced a multitude of situations in which a true response was available, and many situations in which we have had to resort to partial solutions. We have formed many habit patterns, some of which are very adaptive, others of which are less so. These patterns have become automatic. We take them so for granted that even when they cause distress, it often doesn't occur to us that there may be other solutions. For example, it may not occur to the student who plods through all assignments that this approach is maladaptive, that he is suffering understimulation from the drudgery and missing the pleasure that he would experience if he were to approach his assignments with anticipation.

Even when a person is aware that she has acquired a maladaptive habit and wishes to change it, she discovers that this can be very difficult. Why is it so hard for us to rid ourselves of unwanted habits? Once a stimulus has been matched to a response, the two are so closely associated that when the stimulus reappears, it is automatically matched to the same response, even when a better solution is available. A better solution can be matched only if there is an interruption in the previous stimulus-response sequence. A break will occur if a *complex stimulus* appears, one that simultaneously signifies two contradictory solutions. Matching will be momentarily suspended, and the resulting pause will allow an opportunity for a new solution to be matched if one is available.

The student who procrastinates does not know why it is so hard for her to do her work. At some point in the past she responded to anxiety about studying with delay and it became locked in as a habit pattern. Now she always delays. She reads other material, gets herself cups of coffee, and repeatedly sharpens her pencils. If as she begins to sharpen a pencil the sharpener breaks, a complex stimulus is created. For an instant she thinks that she is sharpening her pencil yet simultaneously realizing that she isn't. This pause allows a new solution to be matched with studying: that it needn't always be anxiety-ridden. When a new solution causes a significant change of state, as it does here, repetition will be necessary to decrease its novelty to the point where it can enter awareness. The student experienced a complex stimulus accidentally but an Inner Guide can create them systematically, as needed.

Habit patterns first develop in response to the stimuli provided by our early caretakers. Each time a disturbance such as hunger was solved by provision of food, the relevant solution, we regained a feeling of comfort. We learned that hunger could be solved by eating, and with subsequent experiences of hunger, our perception of the availability of food led to cessation of that discomfort. As our caretakers correctly deduced the sources of our disturbances and provided solutions for them, we learned over time that those solutions, when available, would re-establish comfort. Hunger could be solved by the presence of food, fatigue by the opportunity for sleep, boredom by the availability of toys, danger by removal to a safe place. These solutions are true solutions because they fully alleviate the discomfort caused by the stimulus.

Limit setting may also serve as a true solution for a disturbance. For example, a child may become overly excited by being allowed free rein in a toy store, or may develop a stomach ache if allowed too much candy. The caretaker's empathic responses to these situations, though momentarily experienced as frustrating by the child, will be registered in the mental apparatus as true solutions because they restore the equilibrium. The knowledge of these limits will be available as potential solutions to similar disturbances that occur in the future.

ORIGINS OF DISCOMFORT

To the extent that a child's caretakers are not able to provide appropriate gratification and limit setting, the child will experience ongoing disequilibration and will use whatever solutions are available.

The attitudes and feelings of caretakers toward their children also provide stimuli. A child flourishes in a milieu in which predominantly positive feelings emanate from the caretakers. Each moment is registered in the child's memory with all of the stimuli occurring in that moment, and mental pathways develop consisting of recurring experiences. Just as a pathway containing memories of being hungry and being fed develops, so too do pathways containing memories of being loved, appreciated, and valued. Invariably, there will also be pathways of memories of negative feelings, as when caretakers are angry, critical, or disappointed. But if positive feelings predominate, the child will have a preponderance of such feelings about himself that will contribute toward maintaining a comfortable level of stimulation.

There are a number of ways in which a caretaker can cause a state of ongoing disturbance in a child. Chronic anxiety, anger, or depression will be sensed by the child. If the caretaker is typically preoccupied and emotionally absent from the interaction, the child will experience a state of understimulation and a lack of the emotional interaction that is necessary in order for him to develop his own capacity to relate to others. There are many ways in which a caretaker may unwittingly use a child for his or her own purposes. For instance, a caretaker may erroneously experience a child as inherently "bad," a displacement and partial discharge of feelings the caretaker had developed toward others earlier in life. Or, the caretaker may treat the child as a possession, to replace something that had been missing. A child may be related to in a subtle, sexually stimulating manner, causing an uncomfortable state of overstimulation. With unsatisfied ambition, a caretaker may strive for vicarious satisfaction by urging a child to excel academically, athletically, or artistically.

Children living in poverty or otherwise restricted circumstances often have very limited exposure to the wide variety of experiences that would contribute to the inner network of associations. If they have never been to a zoo, the sight of a dog will not stimulate associated memories of the many animals that are similar. If they have never had the opportunity to paint, the use of a crayon will not evoke memories of other artistic media. They will suffer understimulation not only from the paucity of external stimuli, but from the reduced internal network of associations that is needed to maintain an optimal stimulus level.

Whenever a caretaker uses a child to fulfill his or her own needs in a way that is unrelated to, or antagonistic to, the child's own needs, the child will perceive this experience, either in awareness or subliminally, as an uncomfortable intrusion. A true solution would occur if the caretaker's inappropriate feeling or attitude were to end. Otherwise, the child must develop partial solutions to decrease the discomfort. These developments occur automatically, out of awareness, although the individual may become aware of the end product: the habit pattern.

As an adult, the child may become emancipated from the influence of the caretaker, the external source of the discomfort, but the habit patterns remain because the child has internalized the negative influence. The past thus remains present in the mind. A child who was pressured to excel academically and whose primary partial solution has been to attempt to meet those expectations will, as an adult, retain the memories of those expectations. These memories will cause a continuing pressure to excel. Reverberation between the expectations and the solutions (because they are associatively connected) causes a vicious cycle to form.

The mind also has a tendency to expect from new external figures that which has been experienced from past figures. The individual who was pressured to excel by early caretakers will expect teachers, supervisors, and other authority figures to have the same high expectations because these new figures are associatively connected to the original ones. This pattern is called "transference" by psychodynamically oriented therapists. In fact, the individual will have similar expectations of any new person he encounters because his own internalized high expectation of himself is associatively related to people in general. This phenomenon is generally true. For instance, if an individual is honest, he expects others to be so unless proven otherwise, whereas if he is dishonest, he assumes that others are, too.

An individual's own internally generated feelings may become another source of discomfort. A child's love for his or her parents may become accompanied by sexual feelings that are uncomfortable because they are intense, unsatisfiable, and forbidden. The child may wish to possess the parent exclusively and may become angry, despairing, and envious when this does not occur. These feelings, the love, sexual feelings, anger, despair, and envy, are matched with the partial solutions that most effectively reduce the discomfort. These solutions may include expressing the feelings, fantasying the desired outcome, or directing the feelings toward a different, but associatively related person. Often, the true solution eventually occurs: acceptance of the impossibility of the desire. This result is more difficult to achieve if the parents are not clear that they love and belong to each other, if a parent behaves seductively toward the child or favors the child over other family members, or if a child is reared with only one parent, for whatever reason.

The choice of a false solution may result in significant discomfort. Although it forms an alternative to what may be an extremely distressing stimulus, the other branch of the double pathway, the branch that experiences the distress, is also being experienced out of awareness and is registered in the memory. For example, during a "near death" experience, a hospital patient experiences an episode of cardiac arrest as though he is looking down on it from above. The magnitude and suddenness of this disequilibration are so intense that the false solution of viewing the experience as happening to someone else is more effective than partial solutions, such as: "Maybe my heart will start beating again." This example illustrates the false solution of denial: "Someone else's heart has stopped, not mine."

False solutions usually involve time-limited distress. For all of them there is soon a true solution: the experience is over. There may, nevertheless, be after-effects. Following a "near death" experience, an individual may exhibit avoidance behaviors (for example, avoiding the hospital) and heightened sensitivity to associatively related stimuli (anxiety during subsequent visits to the doctor). Posttraumatic stress disorder is a condition in which a trauma has been so disequilibrating that the after-effects are extensive, very uncomfortable, and interfere with an individual's ability to function adequately. For example, a soldier who has been exposed to unbearable stimuli during military action may suffer prolonged symptoms of anxiety, jumpiness, tremors, nightmares, and flashbacks.

Causes of extreme trauma include pain and other forms of severe physical discomfort, and intense feelings such as fear or rage. If a trauma recurs, the false solution will be repeated. If a trauma recurs many times, the false solution will become a habit pattern. This can be seen in individuals who have dissociative identity disorder. If a child is subjected to repeated extreme abuse, the resulting dissociations that occur will consist of double mental pathways, one of which experiences the trauma out of awareness, the other of which experiences a false solution. Because the sense of identity is ongoing, it will be associatively connected with each of the double experiences, hence, a double identity will develop. Because such individuals typically endure a variety of horrific dangers, different types of false solutions develop, leading to multiple personalities. A current stimulus that is associatively related to a past trauma will evoke the emergence of the relevant personality or personality fragment.

While some unbearable situations lead to false solutions that are obvious, others may be inconspicuous, such as avoidance, or they may even be hidden. For example, if a child experiences intense anxiety, he may dissociate and split off only the feeling. He retains the memory of the situation, but is unaware that he also has a memory pathway, a separate part of himself, containing the intense anxiety. That split-off feeling can subsequently be evoked, seemingly "out of nowhere," by a stimulus that is reminiscent of the original one. For instance, if a young child falls from a window and injures herself, she may retain the memory of the fall but not of her fear. In later years, she may find that she is afraid to be close to a window and remaining unaware of its origin, assume that this fear is normal. When individuals seek psychotherapy, it is important that the therapist be alert for the existence of hidden memory pathways of intense feeling, because such pathways must be recognized in order to be treated.

Other sources of emotional discomfort are the genetically induced vulnerabilities that result in the emergence of certain severe psychiatric disorders, such as schizophrenia, bipolar disorder, and some types of depression. These conditions manifest themselves according to a developmental timetable or when triggered by psychological events.

Some individuals are genetically predisposed to developing an episode of clinical depression following a trauma such as the loss of a relationship. A clinical depression is much different from the unhappiness that is commonly experienced when things don't go as one would wish. In addition to a depressed mood, the symptoms of clinical depression include loss of appetite, significant weight loss, severe insomnia, slowing of speech and physical movement, lessened ability to concentrate, impaired capacity to function in daily life, and preoccupation with certain ideas that are associatively related to the trauma, such as feelings of worthlessness or guilt. This condition, if untreated, frequently progresses to thoughts of suicide and suicide attempts. Such an individual is experiencing a state of intense disequilibration and is focused almost exclusively on this discomfort. He responds with a variety of partial solutions: the expression of the feeling of depression, the attempt to gain control of the situation by assigning blame to himself, and the constant rumination along such lines, overriding even the need for sleep. The undivided focus on the trauma leads to an inability to attend to other needs, or to the matters of everyday life. The intense suffering, with no apparent light at the end of the tunnel is eventually responded to by the idea of death as a solution.

CHANGING UNCOMFORTABLE HABIT PATTERNS

Longstanding, maladaptive habit patterns can be changed only if their origin becomes known and if a true solution is available. For instance, the individual who expects perfection of himself and assumes that all others expect it of him, may come to realize that this expectation originated with a perfectionistic caretaker. He may realize that he has internalized this unnecessary demand, that others don't have the same expectation (or if they do, it is inappropriate), and that he is free to shed this burdensome characteristic.

The individual who has transferred wishes for an exclusive relationship with a parent onto current figures who resemble the parent in various ways may discover that the objects of her desire have been displacements of the original parental figure. She may become aware of a new true solution: that she can find and love a partner who is not a stand-in for the parent but whose qualities she loves.

A person who has experienced severe trauma resulting in a split off memory pathway of terror can undergo a process of integration in which the feeling is re-experienced in manageable doses with awareness of its origin. An individual who suffers an episode of severe depression can, if treated with antidepressant medication, be helped to elucidate the source of the disequilibration and find a true solution.

These disturbances have traditionally been treated with psychoanalysis or psychotherapy, often with excellent results. It is possible, however, to ensure and enhance the effectiveness, and hasten the conclusion of such treatment, by augmenting it through development of an Inner Guide. It would be advisable for a person who is experiencing moderate to severe distress to seek psychotherapeutic help. For those who do not feel in need of this but who wish to shed distressing and maladaptive habit patterns, attain emotional comfort, and maximize their potential for achievement, it is possible to develop an Inner Guide independently, as I did. This book will provide direction on how to do that.

First, however, it will be helpful to consider more examples of maladaptive habit patterns, because many of them tend to go unrecognized as such by their owners. They are silent sources of undefined discomfort and stress.

CHAPTER 3

PARTIAL SOLUTIONS

I HAVE MENTIONED that when a disturbance occurs and a true solution is not available, the mind finds a partial solution. A partial solution cannot end the disturbance but can decrease it.

The earliest partial solutions that are employed by the infant are the inborn responses of vocalization and movement. When an infant is disturbed, it cries and moves its body. In the beginning these responses are simply reflexes. I vividly recall a newborn patient I saw during my rotation on pediatrics during medical school. This infant appeared normal in every respect, both on physical examination and laboratory testing. Reflexes were all normal and the infant cried and moved its arms and legs. When the room was darkened, however, and a flashlight was held to the infant's head, we were amazed to see that the light shone right through its skull. Tragically, there was no brain except for the small hindbrain that controls primitive reflexes. This was a dramatic illustration to me of the extent to which an infant's initial responses to life are merely reflexes.

DEVELOPMENT OF PARTIAL SOLUTIONS

As an infant develops, its disturbances, expressed by crying and bodily movement, are understood by caretakers to represent discomfort and solutions are provided. For example, if an infant is disequilibrated by hunger and cries, it will be fed. It learns that crying is a partial solution for hunger because crying results in the eventual appearance of food. As development proceeds, the infant's crying becomes volitional as it has learned that this will bring the desired result.

The various disturbances that the infant experiences, with their true or partial solutions, form memory pathways. The experiences are stored adjacent to each other like stacks of coins. Because a memory is composed of everything that is present during a moment, the sense of awareness, or identity, becomes a part of each memory. Thus, memories include the sense of self, for instance "I am hungry—I am eating," though the capacity to conceive of "I" is sharpened after the child has acquired language. Also, a feeling is present during each moment, and it too becomes part of the memory. While being fed, the feeling is usually a pleasurable one of having a need satisfied and comfort restored. Expressions of caring and love from the caretaker also become part of the memory.

Being fed and being loved, though different experiences, are associatively related because they occur together. This connection can be useful but, as you may anticipate, can also cause difficulties.

Eating to satisfy hunger becomes a habit pattern. As the child develops, his partial solution of crying and moving his limbs in order to express the distress of hunger becomes elaborated as the development of verbal and motor skills progresses. The infant learns to point or gesture as he cries and when language is acquired he learns to ask for food.

His vocalizations and movements themselves serve as stimuli (because they are perceived, and all perceptions are stimuli). As their novelty wanes with repetition, elaboration occurs.

Simple requests for food become more detailed and specific, not only to acquire the foods his developing taste prefers, but also to provide new types of stimulation that contribute to the maintenance of an optimal level of comfort. As the child develops, he seeks autonomy and competence for the same reasons, both to more effectively assure that his disturbances are solved (his needs and desires met), and to provide an optimal stimulus level for himself with an ever-increasing quantity and complexity of stimuli.

When a habit pattern is first formed it represents the best available solution for a problem. Often it continues to be so, but it becomes maladaptive if it persists as better solutions become available. When a person is hungry, eating is an adaptive solution. If no food is immediately available, he may ask someone for food, cook it himself, or go to a restaurant or grocery store. These are partial solutions, which remain adaptive.

Because eating is associatively connected with the feeling of being cared for, loved, and soothed, however, it may also be used to evoke a sense of that experience. If a person feels tense and no better means of reducing tension is available at that moment, eating remains an adaptive response as long as it doesn't create a greater disequilibration (for instance, a feeling of guilt if he is overweight). If a better solution for a problem exists, however, persistence in eating to reduce the tension becomes maladaptive. It is not solving the problem. Similarly, if a person feels lonely she may eat because the act of eating is associatively connected with the presence of a loving caretaker. To eat because of loneliness is maladaptive because it will not solve the problem.

Thoughts, feelings, and behaviors are adaptive when they represent the best solution for a disturbance. They are maladaptive when they persist in the presence of a better solution. Sometimes a person is aware that a maladaptive response is causing her discomfort. Therapists refer to these responses as *ego-dystonic*, as opposed to maladaptive responses that have become so ingrained as to be unnoticed. They are called *ego-*

syntonic. An Inner Guide identifies and solves all maladaptive responses, including those that are ego-syntonic.

ANXIETY

Ego-dystonic responses to problems cause distress in and of themselves. For example, anxiety is part of a response to danger. It is a component of the "fight or flight" response. When a danger is genuine, this response is adaptive. When a danger is imaginary, however, anxiety is maladaptive because it is uncomfortable and doesn't contribute to a solution. On beginning a new job, an employee may feel some anxiety due to the unknowns she anticipates. Can she do the job well? Will her boss be unpleasant or expect too much? Will her co-workers create problems for her? The anxiety that these uncertainties cause may energize the employee to perform well and should disappear as she becomes accustomed to her new position. This anxiety is normal, and adaptive. On the other hand, many patients seek psychiatric treatment because they have chronic fears that they aren't performing adequately at work, or are afraid of their boss, or feel threatened by aggressive co-workers. Their anxiety is ego-dystonic. They are all too aware of it. Some individuals, however, live with longstanding anxiety that they have become so accustomed to that they assume it as a given. The degree of relief and relaxation that a person feels when having a drink after work is one measure of the degree of anxiety that he lives with.

ANGER

Anger is a component of the "fight" response to a threat. It is useful in situations where an aggressive response would be adaptive, as when a person needs to defend himself against a physical or verbal attack, or against attempted manipulations by others. At times it can be useful as an open display; at other times it serves as a motivator and energizer when a response to danger is needed. In situations where an individual is constrained from responding effectively to a threat, as, for instance, when a child is mistreated by a hostile parent, the feeling of anger constitutes a partial solution. It affords some discharge of tension even when not openly expressed. In such a circumstance, it is adaptive. If, however, an individual suffers from a chronic inhibition of aggression such that he cannot respond to threats that could, in fact, be handled, he may experience bursts of very uncomfortable impotent rage. Or he may feel an ongoing resentment which becomes such second nature that he thinks of it as a given. These, too, are partial solutions: the former ego-dystonic, the latter ego-syntonic. They are maladaptive because a better solution, that of handling the threats, is potentially available. When a person is able to respond to another's aggression, his anger dissipates because the problem has been solved.

Another manifestation of maladaptive anger is that of the individual who is habitually overly aggressive. He is pushy, or bossy, or a bully. He may have had a chronically aggressive parent with whom he identified as a partial solution to the aggression that he, himself, endured. Whatever the original stimulus that evoked this response, he found it helpful to extend its use to additional problems so that it eventually became a generalized response. It is maladaptive because it interferes with his capacity to identify and use true solutions for many of the stimuli he is reacting to, and because the feeling of anger is, itself, an uncomfortable stimulus. Though he causes discomfort in others, he also causes discomfort in himself. He won't seek therapy for this condition because he is unaware that it is a problem. This, too, is an ego-syntonic symptom. Other examples of ego-syntonic character traits that express anger include the person who is hypercritical, both of herself and of others, and one who is passive-aggressive, expressing her anger by responding sluggishly to requests from others.

DEPRESSION

Depression, another partial solution, is a discharge of feeling in response to a loss. Some losses are obvious, such as the death or departure of a relative or friend, loss of a job or of an anticipated promotion, a reversal of financial fortune or social position, a move, the loss of a talent or capability (due to accident, illness or aging), an inability to achieve an important aspiration or a loss in an important competition. A depressive response to a sudden, significant loss may be quite marked. Its severity will depend on the extent of the disequilibration. It will also depend on how many previous losses have been experienced, because as a partial solution is repeated, it must be intensified or elaborated in order to retain its power. Repeated losses will result in increasingly strong depressive responses.

An ongoing feeling of depression can result from the accumulation of many small losses, especially during childhood. A variety of deficiencies in a child's caretakers may cause this to happen. A depressed or otherwise preoccupied mother may be unable to attend to her child's need to relate to her and to have her relate to him. Each time the child tries to engage her and fails, he experiences a loss. A mother who sees her child as inherently "bad" will also disappoint this child as he tries to please her. A father who wants to have his own needs met through his child may well find the child deficient for that purpose. That child will have an ongoing feeling of loss, both of his father's pleasure in him and of his own satisfaction with himself. If a child is impaired in some way, she will have difficulty performing up to her own expectations or those of others. She may suffer rejection from her peer group or family as well as experiencing a deficit in her own self-esteem. A person who has developed an ongoing feeling of depression will have some awareness of it, but often doesn't fully realize the extent of her discomfort.

EGO-DYSTONIC SYMPTOMS

When a person seeks therapy, it is most often because he has become aware of an ego-dystonic symptom that is causing obvious distress. In addition to feelings of anxiety, anger, and depression, an individual may come for help with phobias, obsessions or compulsions, or other symptoms of which he is painfully aware. Many physical symptoms are found to be not of organic causation but an indirect expression of feelings. Headache, various other kinds of pain, gastrointestinal disorders, and sexual dysfunction are a few of the symptoms that may have a psychological origin. Or, a person might find that she has developed a pattern of saying or doing things that she later (or simultaneously) regrets. Some individuals develop a vague but alarming feeling of "falling apart" or find themselves feeling increasingly detached either from the world around them or from their own sense of self.

Less frequently, an individual may seek therapy because of an increasing realization that she is failing to achieve important goals. She may experience a pattern of difficulty in succeeding at work or a series of failed relationships.

EGO-SYNTONIC SYMPTOMS

People tend not to seek help for ego-syntonic traits, however, because they don't realize that these are problematic. They have become second nature as in the following examples.

Amanda is very thoughtful toward others, so much so that she takes care of them at her own expense. Though employed in a demanding job, she also does most of the housework, and is very sensitive to her husband's needs. He does not reciprocate. Many women would be aware of this inequity. They would protest and refuse to tolerate it for long, but Amanda assumes that this is the way things are. She doesn't know why she is feeling so "stressed out" and wonders what is the matter with her that she can't keep up with everything. When it is suggested to her that she is doing too much for others and not enough for herself, her response is to feel that it would be very selfish of her to put herself first.

Ben has become increasingly rigid and controlling over the years. At work he had expected perfection from his employees and at home he had imposed his will on his family. His wife had acquiesced to his overbearing attitude and his son had struggled to attain a sense of autonomy. Oblivious to the discomfort that he had caused his family, Ben felt that his perfectionism was a positive trait. After retirement, his focus narrowed to his home where he has become increasingly preoccupied with the specifics of its maintenance. Unaware that his rigidity is a partial solution for underlying anxiety, he is unable to expand his interests and seek pleasure in the many opportunities for new experiences that are potentially available to him.

Charles feels resentful toward his boss and toward co-workers who take advantage of him. He fumes silently at work and complains unendingly to his family and friends. They agree with him that he is being abused and offer various suggestions for dealing with these problems, none of which does he try. It seems as though he would rather complain than assert himself. His passivity, with subsequent resentment, is a partial solution to situations that he finds threatening. Although he isn't content, he appears to take his dissatisfaction for granted. He doesn't know that it could be possible to handle his problems more effectively and achieve a sense of mastery over his work situation.

Dorothy is working at a job that is beneath her capabilities. Having been given insufficient support by her parents while growing up, and with low expectations for her on their part, she has assumed that she is doing the best that she can for herself. She finds that those around her are less competent than she is but doesn't put two and two together to realize that she is capable of much more. She feels a vague discontent but doesn't understand its source. She has responded to the distress of insufficient recognition and support by acquiescing to her parents' view of her.

Evan feels dependent on his mentor, not only for information and guidance, but also as a source of emotional support. Without quite realizing it, he views his mentor as one who has the power to take care of him as a parent would. When an opportunity came for Evan to take a better position at a different company, he chose not to take it. He wasn't aware that his dependence on his mentor was the reason why he couldn't move. As with Dorothy, he had experienced insufficient support from his parents as a child and his partial solution has involved attaching himself to figures who are more giving.

Flora, though she has an excellent income, is chronically worried about whether she has enough money and therefore focuses single-mindedly on accumulating more. In so doing, she also has come to value wealth as a source of status. It has become so important to her that she hasn't made time for other things in life. She would have liked to have married and had children, but it is now too late, at least for children. Marriage remains something that she hopes will happen "someday." This is unlikely because her focus on accumulating money has intensified over time. It has served as a partial solution for underlying distress of which she is only dimly aware.

Grace's life is full of activity, and every minute is occupied. In addition to her work, she responds to her friends' requests for help and extends herself on their behalf. She plans many projects for herself, some of which she is able to complete, others not. She is so busy that she talks quickly, moves quickly, and makes decisions quickly. It is difficult for her to think beyond the moment or to make long-term plans. She isn't able to read anything of length, though she does read in order to fall asleep because otherwise she would have insomnia. This perpetual motion serves as a partial solution for her underlying anxiety.

As partial solutions become habit patterns, their novelty wanes. To continue providing partial relief for disturbances, they must become more pronounced and/or more elaborated over time. Ben, the man who is rigid, will become even more so. In focusing on the maintenance of his home, he will spend more and more time on the tasks of upkeep, such as minor repairs, lawn care, and so forth. He will perform these chores with increasing perfectionism. Grace, the woman who needs to be active, will find more projects to begin but will leave unfinished, as she increasingly overcommits herself.

Some of the traits that become maladaptive partial solutions seem, at first sight, very positive. Isn't it good to help others? Yes, when this quality evolves as an elaboration of taking care of oneself and after one's own needs have been met. Amanda, the woman who cares for her husband at her own expense feels "stressed." If she took care of her own needs (which would include providing herself with a reasonably caring husband), she would then feel comfortable and could give to him without strain (as he would to her). In so doing, she would provide new stimulation for herself, which would contribute toward maintaining an optimal level of comfort.

Aren't there times when tendencies such as Ben's, that is, narrowing of focus and striving for perfection, are advantageous? Yes, these qualities are important for those who have exacting tasks to master. A musician, a dancer, a surgeon, all need to concentrate intensely on their area of expertise in order to achieve excellence.

How can you know whether a trait you have is healthy or maladaptive, especially when it has become second nature and seems "normal?" Occasionally, someone might comment to you that you seem excessively active, or overly conscientious, or modest to a fault. But this characterization is not necessarily reliable as it might come from someone who is too much the opposite. In fact, it may not be possible for you to decide whether a given characteristic of yours is maladaptive.

If you use maladaptive traits that seem "normal" to you and that don't feel problematic, why should you concern yourself with them? They are harmful because they interfere with your capacity to solve problems and leave you burdened with various symptoms, including unnecessary anxiety, anger, and depression. Although these feelings may be partially or even wholly unrecognized, they can nevertheless exert a very damaging effect on your ability to achieve and maintain emotional comfort.

Most emotional distress can be eliminated if we are able to find true solutions for our problems. Then our energies will be liberated and we will be able to think clearly, feel free, and fully enjoy life. We will maintain an optimal level of comfort, not by repeating maladaptive partial solutions, but by elaborating true solutions. Amanda, if she took care of her own needs first, would experience a refreshing and stimulating wish to give to others. Ben, if he found a true solution for his underlying anxieties, would seek new sources of stimulation and expand his interests. Charles, if he overcame his fear of being assertive, would find himself able to pursue his goals with confidence. Dorothy, if she freed herself from her unrealistically low self-assessment, would be free to develop her talents. So, too, the underlying distress of the others, and in fact of most people, could be left behind if they became able to find true solutions for their problems.

When liberated from faulty solutions, we can develop our talents and capabilities painlessly by expecting more and more of ourselves at a pace that provides pleasurable stimulation and that, therefore, is optimally comfortable. Moreover, learning that occurs in this way is better remembered and used because it is uncontaminated by discomfort. We can enrich our lives by magnifying simple pleasures into multiple and complex ones, undiluted by extraneous concerns. And, as we attain emotional comfort, we will have more to give: to our loved ones, to our work, and to society.

CHAPTER 4

FALSE SOLUTIONS

WHEN A DISTURBANCE occurs for which there is no true or partial solution, the mind chooses a false solution. Although some such situations are relatively inconsequential as, when one initially negates the existence of an impending cold, others are quite extreme, as when a patient dissociates while experiencing a cardiac arrest.

As with partial solutions, a newly chosen false solution is adaptive. It protects the individual from extremes of overstimulation whether it is positive, as when a student initially disbelieves that he has won a prize, or negative, as when a woman in labor does not feel the intense pain.

Most situations resulting in a false solution are short-lived. The patient's heart begins beating again. The student's overstimulation wanes with the repeated realization that he has won the prize. The woman's labor ends with the birth of her baby. The mental split that has occurred during the dissociation, with the simultaneous creation of two separate mental pathways, ends. One pathway has registered the distress; the

44

other has experienced the false solution. The pathway of distress remains out of awareness and the individual has no memory of it. Instead, he remembers the false solution. The patient remembers that he was looking down from above. The student who won the prize remembers that there were moments during which he couldn't believe he had won. The woman remembers that she felt no pain. The pathway of distress, though it remains out of awareness, nevertheless exists. It contains not only the event and its accompanying feeling but also the sense of identity. "My heart stopped beating." "I won the prize." "I felt intense pain."

Subsequently, stimuli that are reminiscent of the split-off distress may re-evoke the double pathway. As the man who suffered a cardiac arrest later drives by the hospital in which it occurred, he may remember having looked down from above at the "stranger" whose heart had stopped. He will also re-experience, out of awareness, the knowledge that his heart had stopped beating and the accompanying anxiety.

FLASHBACKS

Because the creation and maintenance of split-off mental pathways require intense effort by the mind, bits and pieces of the experience may slip into awareness. These are called flashbacks. They occur when the stress due to maintaining the split is greater than would be the case if the split were ended. This situation can occur when an individual perceives a complex stimulus related to the trauma. It causes a pause, during which the false solution can be replaced by the memory of the original disturbance. If an individual who has amnesia for an attack revisits the scene of this event, the location may serve as a complex stimulus, as it signifies both a benign and a dangerous place. During the pause, the memory of the attack or aspects of it may come into awareness. It feels as though it is happening in the here and now because, as it has been sequestered out of awareness, the individual is unaware that it is a past event.

The most dramatic type of flashback is that in which a traumatic event is relived in its entirety. More often, a partial flashback occurs. This consists of that part of the split-off experience that is bearable at that point in time. Partial flashbacks may consist of sensory aspects of the trauma. One person may see the scene of her rape, another may hear the sound of bombs. More often, the aspect that enters awareness is a portion of the feeling such as anxiety, or the physical sensation such as pain. A woman who has amnesia for the experience of being stabbed by an attacker may feel anxious when seeing someone who resembles that person or, upon being touched where she was stabbed, feel pain in that spot.

There is a tendency for stimuli that resemble the traumatic stimulus to also serve as triggers that re-evoke elements of a flashback. The woman who was stabbed may come to feel anxious at the sight of any kind of knife. If she was attacked at dusk, she may come to feel anxious in the evenings and this may extend to fear of the entire night. The degree to which these aftereffects of the trauma become generalized depends on many factors.

While dissociation is a useful protection from overstimulation when it first comes into being, its aftereffects are maladaptive. It is not necessary or useful to experience uncomfortable flashbacks unless their occurrence results in integration of the split-off pathway. An Inner Guide is aware of split-off pathways and works to integrate them.

DISSOCIATION

A dissociative disorder can take a number of forms. When double pathways have become very extensive, an individual will suffer from dissociative identity disorder. There are several forms of dissociation that have more limited effects. A person who has an episode of amnesia has split off and blocked from awareness a portion of his self-knowledge. At times, such a person may travel to a different location and take on a new identity, remaining oblivious to his previous self-knowledge for a period of time. This is known as a fugue state. "Conversion" symptoms, which involve the loss or alteration of a physical function, such as psychologically caused blindness or paralysis, also result from the formation of a double pathway in response to a trauma. More commonly, an individual may experience depersonalization, a state in which he feels detached from himself, as though he is observing himself as he would another (as with the patient who experienced cardiac arrest). Or he may feel like a robot, or as though he were in a dream. In fact, dreams are instances of partial or, occasionally, full flashbacks. Trance states, hypnotic states, and daydreaming are also the result of dissociation.

TRAUMATIC EVENTS

Traumatic events such as attacks, accidents, and natural catastrophes (earthquakes, tornadoes and so forth) are, unfortunately, all too common. But by far the most frequent traumas are those undergone by young children when they experience situations that cause unbearably intense feeling. For a variety of reasons, young children are more vulnerable than older people. They are less able to handle extremes of feeling because the repetitions that will result in decreasing disequilibration have been fewer. A child who learns that his parents prefer a sibling may feel devastated and overcome with despair and rage. Because of their limited knowledge and experience, children are more apt to misunderstand communications and situations, which can lead to erroneous impressions of danger. For instance, a child who overhears his parents talking about a faraway war may assume that it will endanger his family. Many things appear larger and more powerful to children because children are small and relatively helpless. A big dog, a loud motorcycle, a carnival ride all may be terrifying. New situations are more disequilibrating because of their novelty. For example, the strangeness of a clown, however benign, may frighten a child. Because there are so many possibilities for trauma to occur, dissociative experiences in children are common. Also, individuals who are innately very sensitive will be especially susceptible to traumatic overstimulation.

Will all early dissociative experiences result in extensive aftereffects? No, the majority will not. All will, however, cause the formation of a split-off pathway that will be triggered by a relevant stimulus. The child who was traumatized by a big dog will have an aversion to big dogs, because the sight of another will trigger the split-off reaction of anxiety. This sensitivity will continue, perhaps until she has grown enough so that big dogs no longer seem so huge to her. A large network of associated stimuli will not develop because she won't encounter big dogs very often. In contrast, a girl who is repeatedly beaten by her alcoholic mother may have many moments when she splits off anxiety. The more often this happens, the larger the network of associated triggers will become. She may find herself feeling anxious in the presence of other mothers, or when seeing another child scolded, or even on coming home from school every day.

Every young child occasionally experiences fright over something that an adult knows to be harmless, or has a temper tantrum over an issue that appears trivial to others. The child may remember the event and the feeling but split off the excess emotion that is unbearable. When this occurs, neither he nor his parents will be aware that a portion of the feeling has been split off.

Many people have experienced multiple episodes of this kind of dissociation as children. As the person develops, these pathways form reservoirs of feeling that will be triggered by an increasing number of related stimuli, including current feeling states. That is, when such a person becomes anxious for any reason, that anxiety will trigger the hidden reservoir of anxiety. The result will be a response that is out of proportion to the current stimulus. For instance, a person with split-off anxiety may feel excessively anxious if he thinks that he has displeased his boss. Or he may find himself unable to rise to an adult challenge if a split-off pathway of anxiety from his childhood feels "I'm too little to be able to do that." A person with split-off anger may respond to an annoying driver with road rage. A person who has split-off depression may, on seeing a sad movie, feel so distraught that she has to leave in the middle. Some of these flashbacks will be ego-syntonic; for instance, an individual with road rage is often unaware that this is abnormal. Other flashbacks may be ego-dystonic; for example, the woman who leaves in the middle of a sad movie may realize that her reaction is excessive, without understanding why.

When a person has experienced a number of dissociations and developed a large network of related stimuli, the frequency with which they occur may result in an ongoing low-grade feeling of anxiety, anger, or depression. For instance, the girl who was repeatedly beaten by her alcoholic mother may come to feel chronic anxiety, anger, and despair. She won't realize the significance of these feelings because they will have become second nature.

When an overwhelming experience has been completely split off, the false solution may consist of an alternative memory, such as the impression that someone else's heart has stopped beating, or it may consist of complete amnesia. When the latter occurs, the person also develops what has been called "amnesia for his amnesia"; that is, he doesn't remember that he doesn't remember a certain period of time. He may recall a memory as, for instance, "I was taken into the woods by this man...later, when I was in the back yard, Mom called me in to dinner," with no recognition that a time gap occurred.

When a trauma has been completely split off, evidence of it may be available. The man who saw the "stranger's" cardiac arrest will be told about his own. The woman who was stabbed will be aware of her hospitalization and her scar. However, when a trauma has been partially split off, when only the overwhelming feeling has been relegated to a hidden pathway, the dissociation is fully concealed. The individual remembers the event and the accompanying feeling but has no way of knowing that an additional portion of the feeling has been split off. The girl may remember that her mother beat her and that she was scared, but be unaware that she was petrified with fear.

Certain false solutions, such as those that result in impairment of physical functions, are ego-dystonic. A person experiencing difficulty with vision or mobility, for example, will seek treatment. Flashbacks, too, if sufficiently frequent and intense, will lead an individual to seek help. Certain types of symptoms, however, will often be kept hidden. An individual with dissociative identity disorder who "hears" voices in her head (the voices of one or more of her alternate personalities) or becomes aware that she is losing time (which will occur when an "alter" is in control) may fear that she is "crazy." She won't want to tell anyone. In fact, she doesn't want to know herself because she finds it frightening. If she sees evidence of the activity of her alters, such as rearrangement of her possessions or unfamiliar clothing in her closet, she will tend to disregard it. The great majority of false solutions, however, are ego-syntonic, whether they consist of an alternative memory, "I saw someone having a cardiac arrest," or amnesia.

You may be wondering whether you have split-off pathways of distressing emotion. You probably do. Who among us has been spared from all early traumas? Not all instances of early fears, rages, and grief result in split-off pathways, but the most traumatic of them are likely candidates for dissociation.

Significance of Traumas

You may also wonder whether whatever dissociations you experienced as a young child are having a significant effect on your life now. Isolated traumas resulting from the vulnerability of early childhood, such as being frightened by a big dog, are unlikely to cause distress in adulthood because they tend not to become associatively connected with a large number of related stimuli and because such experiences tend to become integrated (no longer split off) as the individual develops. If a person, who was frightened by a big dog when small re-encounters one at a later age, feels anxiety but then realizes that the dog is not dangerous, integration of the split-off memory will occur.

A truly dangerous event, on the other hand, is less likely to become integrated because it cannot be repeated as a benign experience. If it is an isolated occurrence, however, and unlikely to recur, it may have no impact on the individual's future comfort. For instance, a little girl playing by the edge of an ice-covered river, fell in. She was able to grab the root of a tree at water's edge and hung on until her playmate fetched her mother, who pulled her out. Though she hadn't fallen in deeper than her waist, her subjective experience and subsequent memory was that she went fully underwater and was intrigued by the fish she saw swimming about. This hallucination was a false solution to the extreme disequilibration caused by the danger of drowning. This trauma has never become integrated. The fear remains split off and to this day her memory is only of the fishes. There are no uncomfortable consequences for her. The fear of drowning did not generalize to related situations because the circumstances of the trauma were unique and because that situation will not occur again.

The probability that a dissociated trauma will cause later discomfort will depend on the extent to which a network of associated stimuli is generated and on whether or not a dissociation can become spontaneously integrated. The girl who was repeatedly terrorized by her alcoholic mother will develop a large network. There are more stimuli linked to a mother than to a big dog or to a mishap on a frozen river. Integration will be unlikely because she will have internalized the frightening stimulus, so the present will not seem like a contrast with the past, as is the case with the girl who could outgrow her fear of big dogs. She will be susceptible to feelings of anxiety, anger, and despair. Because these feelings are disequilibrating themselves, her mind will seek ways, partial solutions, to decrease the pain. She may follow her mother's example and resort to alcohol. She may discharge tension as an adult by striking out at her own child. Or she may identify with children and gain vicarious satisfaction by treating them kindly.

Many people, unfortunately, have been the victims of overt abuse. Many others have experienced less serious, and less obvious, trauma. The various ways in which parents may fail their children, described in chapters 2 and 3, can also cause dissociation. When such failures stimulate very intense emotion in a child, partial solutions may be inadequate and the child's mind may need to find a false solution.

SOLVING FALSE SOLUTIONS

How can one tell whether a habitual feeling of anxiety, anger, or sadness is a partial solution or a false one? This distinction can be very difficult, even in psychoanalysis or psychotherapy. Consider the following clinical example.

Henry seeks therapy because he is afraid of his boss. In addition to the discomfort caused by his fear, his work has suffered to the extent that he has missed out on a promotion. He also feels inhibited with women.

During his early years, his father, who was in the military, was absent, for extended periods of time. His Oedipal feelings toward his mother, that is, his wishes to possess her sexually and exclusively, were intensified because, with his father absent, his mother seemed more available to him. Yet this situation was frightening because of its intensity. Although, on the one hand, he was glad that his father was absent, he nevertheless missed him and felt angry with him for being away. Each time his father returned home, Henry feared retribution, imagining that his father would be able to perceive his desire for his mother. This situation interfered with his capacity to resolve his Oedipal feelings by accepting the impossibility of his desire. These feelings became transferred onto the adult figures in his life. He was afraid of his boss, as of his father, and felt inhibited with women, who represented his forbidden mother.

In treatment, Henry develops transferences toward his therapist. He experiences her as he did his mother; he falls in love with her. The therapist provides an interpretation: she tells him that he is experiencing her as he did his mother when he was young, but that she is his therapist, not his mother. She is unavailable to him, as was his mother but, as an adult, he is now able to seek a woman in his current life to love. It is important that the therapist provide this interpretation while he is experiencing loving feelings toward her so that there will be a confluence of past (the feelings) and present (the relationship with his therapist). The therapist also interprets his transference to his boss and if there is evidence (if he fears her) a paternal transference toward her. Because these interpretations will lead to great change, they are very overstimulating and must be repeated a number of times before they can take effect.

In many cases, such interpretations are successful and a patient who has come for treatment with Oedipal problems no longer feels inhibited with women or afraid of men. But Henry's fears continue. The therapist provides other interpretations for which she sees clinical evidence. He may feel angry with her (as a transference figure representing his mother) for seeming to be available, for seeming oblivious to his feelings, and so forth. Other problems may complicate the picture, and the therapist provides all the additional interpretations for which there is evidence. His problems continue. The therapist wonders, "Does he need still more repetition of the interpretations already provided?" or "Is there a problem that has not yet surfaced?" or "Am I missing something because of unanalyzed problems of my own?"

There is another possibility. Henry may have split off a portion of the emotions he felt as a young boy, emotions that were unbearably intense. He may have developed hidden pathways of dissociated fright, rage, or despair. If so, interpretations of the transference can serve as new stimuli that actually add to the reservoir of painful feelings. But if the therapist is aware of the possibility of hidden pathways, she can make an additional interpretation to that effect. While he is in the throes of his unrequited love for her, she can say that not only is he re-experiencing with her the feelings he had toward his mother when he was young, but that the present situation is stimulating a split-off reservoir of anguish which originated because his feelings for his mother were unbearably intense. That split-off part of him, a "young part," needs to understand that those days are over and that although he can't have her, as he couldn't have his mother, there are women in his life now whom he can have. This interpretation creates an associative link between the hidden pathway and the true solution.

Transference is a partial solution, as are the accompanying feelings. But if, due to their intensity, a dissociation has been necessary, the unbearable feelings become split off, forming a separate pathway. This reservoir of intense, painful feeling is an area of special sensitivity that will be triggered by any relevant stimulus. How can this situation be resolved? As with Henry, if an individual experiences both the split-off pathway (the intense feeling) and the false solution (the unawareness of the cause of this feeling) simultaneously and is provided at that moment with an explanation of the split-off pathway, this moment will form a new pathway that will consist of the totality of that experience. The two pathways and the understanding of them will be combined. This is an integration.

Integrations sometimes occur spontaneously, as with a girl who overcomes her fear of big dogs, but more often than not the necessary components (that is, the two pathways and the understanding of their origin) do not occur simultaneously. Psychoanalysis or psychoanalytic psychotherapy can provide the necessary conditions for integrations to take place.

As you develop your Inner Guide, integrations will occur automatically, often without even entering your awareness. If you are experiencing moderate or severe emotional distress, you should seek psychotherapeutic treatment and work on developing your Inner Guide in that context. How can you tell whether your distress is "moderate or severe?" That can best be discussed after the technique for attaining emotional comfort has been described.

* * *

We have surveyed the various types of emotional distress that can occur in an individual. A few of them are caused in part by hereditary factors that result in neurophysiological dysfunction. Most, however, arise from the environment in which an individual develops. They are the partial and false solutions that, though initially necessary, have become maladaptive. As an Inner Guide develops, these habit patterns are gradually abolished.

In order to benefit from the use of self-hypnosis to achieve emotional comfort, it is necessary to know what the Inner Guide consists of, and how it develops. In my own experience, I stumbled on it by chance and it took me several years to fully understand it. The explanation given in the next chapter will provide you with the understanding that you will need in order to most efficiently bring your own Inner Guide into existence.

CHAPTER 5

TRUE SOLUTIONS

EVERY TIME A stimulus causes a disequilibration, the mind matches that stimulus with the most satisfactory solution. When a true solution is available, it will be chosen. The disturbance will end and a state of regained comfort will occur. From infancy onward we have had innumerable experiences that have resulted in the restoration of comfort. Whenever we were hungry and then fed, or cold and then covered with a blanket, or overstimulated and then helped to calm down, we regained a state of comfort. As we have developed, we have learned how to find and use these true solutions ourselves. All of these experiences are retained in the memory.

When a memory is stored, its various components are saved in their corresponding pathways. For example, if one is frightened by a large dog, the fear is stored in a pathway consisting of other memories of fear. The shape, color, and other characteristics of the memory are each retained with like characteristics in their individual pathways. When stimulated, the memory is reassembled from its components.

When true solutions are stored, the feeling of regained comfort is saved with similar past memories. Thus, a memory pathway consisting of a sense of well-being is formed. This is the primordial *Inner Guide*. It is associatively connected to all of the various true solutions that have been used in the past and it has the potential for providing true solutions for present and future disturbances. It can allow a person to attain maximal emotional comfort. How might this happen?

HYPNOSIS

Hypnosis has been described as a state in which a dissociation, or mental split, occurs. A subject is told to focus intensely on one thing, such as a spot on the wall, and to disregard all other stimuli. By so doing, the subject enters a state in which he may respond to suggestions automatically, without willing them himself. For instance, he may be told that his arm will spontaneously rise, and it does. Or that his eyes will spontaneously close, and they do. Hypnosis is often used to assist a person in becoming oblivious to pain or to change an unwanted habit. For instance, some dentists use hypnosis to provide anesthesia for dental procedures. And some individuals have stopped smoking through suggestions provided during hypnosis.

How can we understand these phenomena? What is hypnosis? If a person wishes to be hypnotized, he will want to follow the hypnotist's instructions. If he is told, "Your eyes will spontaneously close," this implies that his eyes will be closed by a part of his mind that he does not feel to be a part of his own identity. It is as though someone else is closing his eyes. As all of his existing mental pathways are associated with his sense of identity, a false solution must occur. A new pathway must be initiated in which his sense of identity is negated or denied. This new pathway, not part of his own sense of identity, forms an "Other." This occurs out of awareness. It is the "Other's" pathway that closes the eyes or raises the arm. Although the "Other" originates as a false solution, it becomes a true solution because it provides the response that ends the subject's disequilibration. It has fulfilled the subject's wish to be hypnotized. It demonstrates this by closing the eyes, raising the arm, or performing whatever action the hypnotist has suggested. This occurs as the unchanging spot loses its novelty and its stimulatory capacity, leaving the wish to be hypnotized as the most powerful stimulus and allowing the "Other" to become dominant.

Self-Hypnosis

Inner conversations, or exchanges of thoughts, occur in the mind. For example, when an individual who is dieting is offered a piece of cake, one part of the mind thinks, "Don't eat that cake, it has too many calories," but another part may think, "I'm going to eat it anyway." These inner conversations arise from different mental pathways. In self-hypnosis, different pathways are engaged when an individual serves as both hypnotist and subject. One pathway contains the sense of identity and the wish to be hypnotized. The other pathway will contain the "Other." A person may use this technique to achieve a state of relaxation or peace, to feel a sense of oneness with the universe or a sense of connection to some aspect of her spiritual life, to gain access to otherwise forgotten memories or to an internal sense of wisdom, to achieve relief from certain symptoms of illness, or to change a habit. "Meditation," which is used for some of the same purposes, occurs by means of the same mechanism. In meditation, focus on breathing, a repeated word, or imagery serves to diminish other stimuli just as focusing on a spot on the wall does. The wished for "Other," whether simply a feeling state or a distinct entity, becomes dominant.

When a person begins self-hypnosis her mind combines the newly generated "Other" and the desired effect, such as a feeling of peace, in response to her wish. If the wish is for a spiritual guide or a source of wisdom, the "Other" is combined with the thoughts and feelings that would contribute to the assembly of such an entity.

One has to have experiences in order to develop a mind. A mind is composed of stimulus-response pathways. As stimuli repeatedly occur and are matched with responses, the pathways enlarge and phenomena that are temporally contiguous form associative networks. A sense of identity is one of the components of these pathways. Just as an individual's mind expands with experience, so too does the "Other's." Over time, with repeated use of self-hypnosis, the wished-for creation develops a sense of its own identity and enlarges as it becomes associated with an expanding network of thoughts and feelings.

WHAT IS THE INNER GUIDE?

How does an Inner Guide differ from an internal source of wisdom that can be consulted for solutions to problems? If, as entering a self-hypnotic state, a person's wish is not for the solution to a specific problem but for emotional comfort, the mind will assemble an "Other" that is composed of a sense of its own identity, an intention of providing emotional comfort, and the pathway of well-being that has grown from all the past experiences of regained comfort. This entity is, itself, free of discomfort. Its subjective experience is of serenity and well-being and it is motivated to help the person achieve that same state. Because it is composed of stimuli and their true solutions, it has no ongoing disequilibration as would occur with partial and false solutions. Lacking that "static," it is able to perceive all the sources of a person's discomfort, including sources that she herself isn't aware of. The Inner Guide identifies solutions for these discomforts but has other tasks to fulfill before the solutions can be implemented.

Although a new and better solution may be identified, the mind continues to choose the one that is already linked to the stimulus, unless an interruption occurs between the stimulus and the original response. Then, and only then, can a new response be selected. In order for an interruption to occur, the Inner Guide must create a complex stimulus, one that signifies two contradictory meanings. Because the mind cannot immediately respond to both meanings, a pause occurs, which provides the opportunity for a new response to be chosen.

For example, a woman may have developed a partial solution for loneliness by turning to food, which has been connected since infancy with being loved. This dependence on food may result in a weight gain that causes her distress about her appearance. A true solution for her loneliness would be to find someone to share her life with but this becomes more difficult as she gains more and more weight. Not only does her mind need to identify the true solution, it also needs to interrupt the previous solution of overeating, which has been locked in as her response to loneliness. A complex stimulus that is associatively related to eating must occur.

Suppose that one evening as she sets the table she forgets to include a fork. When she sits down to eat she is confronted with a complex stimulus: the place setting suggests that she can eat, but the missing fork indicates that she cannot. She will momentarily be startled and immobilized, and during that moment, her mind can choose a new solution for the loneliness: to eat healthily and to take advantage of current opportunities to find a partner. These mental activities occur extremely rapidly, and out of awareness. The Inner Guide, aware of this possibility for attaining emotional comfort, can cause a fork to be forgotten just as it can cause an arm to spontaneously rise or eyes to spontaneously close. It uses such devices to implement the true solutions that it has discovered for attaining emotional comfort. In this instance the woman can overcome both her loneliness and her distress at being overweight.

Does one incident of a forgotten fork lead to a changed habit? No, there is another complication to be overcome. When a true solution to a problem is selected, the implications are so overstimulating that the mind must protect itself by initially remaining unaware of the new solution (another use of a false solution). Gradually, as the new solution is repetitively identified, the overstimulation wanes and the new solution can then enter awareness and be implemented.

Changes for the better can and do occur in people without their having developed an Inner Guide whenever the necessary conditions have been met. These changes occur by chance. The advantage of developing an Inner Guide is that true solutions will be implemented systematically and efficiently. The Inner Guide's purpose in life is to end emotional discomfort in the person it is a part of, and it has the capability to do that.

Although we may create an Inner Guide simply by wishing for it, we can only benefit from its existence through the use of self-hypnosis. It is important that we understand the concept of the Inner Guide and that we wish for it to help us. As we sit in a quiet room and focus on a spot on the wall with the wish that our eyes would spontaneously close, we are minimizing both the external stimuli of perceptions and the internal stimuli of our usual thoughts and feelings. As we continue to focus on the spot its novelty wanes and its stimulatory capacity therefore weakens. There comes a moment when the wish that our eyes would spontaneously close becomes the most disequilibrating stimulus. At this moment, the eyes will close and the body and mind will relax. We have entered the self-hypnotic state; that is, a state in which the stimuli that are most disequilibrating are those that can best be responded to by the Inner Guide. The Inner Guide thus becomes dominant. Because it is not part of our sense of identity, we don't experience it as part of our mind; we only experience its effects. It remains dominant until a stimulus that overrides its activity, a stimulus that is best responded to by our own sense of identity (such as a doorbell, or the knowledge that it is time to make dinner) occurs. At this point, as we respond to such a stimulus we resume dominance and the self-hypnotic state ends.

In the self-hypnotic state during which the Inner Guide's pathway is dominant, what is occurring in the pathway that contains our own sense of identity? What is our subjective experience? No longer needing to focus on the spot, we resume our usual thoughts and feelings. If our internal stimuli are sufficient, we may continue to think and feel until a stimulus occurs that requires us to end the self-hypnotic session. If our internal stimuli wane sufficiently, however, we enter a state of unawareness, as though we were asleep. This is how "hypnosis" got its name. It is not the same as sleep, however, because the Inner Guide remains aware.

What is the nature of the Inner Guide's activity during self-hypnosis? And why is self-hypnosis necessary in order for the Inner Guide to be effective? Because the Inner Guide's purpose is to solve problems that interfere with emotional comfort, it chooses solutions to problems as they occur. Because these solutions are often too over-stimulating to enter awareness, however, it is necessary that they be repeated until their novelty wanes. For example, the lonely woman's realization that there was a solution to her loneliness and to her weight problem represented an overwhelming shift in her life situation. As the Inner Guide assumes dominance during self-hypnosis, it experiences the feeling of being real. Therefore, it experiences stimuli and its responses to them as perceptions. Because perceptions are more intense than their corresponding thoughts and feelings, they cause more reverberation of the stimulus-response cycles and, therefore, more repetition of the new solutions. Significant changes require this degree of repetition in order for their novelty to wane to a point at which they are no longer too disequilibrating to enter awareness.

Because of the intense impact that important new solutions have on us, we tend to become aware of them gradually. The lonely woman will change her diet one step at a time. Because her Inner Guide works silently, she may not realize why she feels motivated to make these changes. Sometimes one understands only in retrospect that a major transformation has occurred because of the influence of the Inner Guide.

Although the Inner Guide works silently, directing one's mind to true solutions which can then be carried out, it can make its presence known when necessary once the novelty of its existence has waned sufficiently so that we can tolerate awareness of its presence. The Inner Guide may then converse with us by means of finger signals, handwriting, and inner thought. Occasionally, it may decide not to communicate for an extended time if it determines that this would be most efficient.

* * *

The preceding chapters have comprised a description of the new theory of mental functioning that I developed to explain the events that occurred when I began to do self-hypnosis. By reading them, you have registered them in your memory for your Inner Guide's use. You are now ready to develop your own Inner Guide.

CHAPTER 6

THE DAVIS TECHNIQUE FOR ATTAINING EMOTIONAL COMFORT

IT ISN'T NECESSARY for you to remember all that you have read. All you need to keep in mind is the understanding that *the Inner Guide consists of three things: (1) a sense of its own identity, (2) the wish to help you attain emotional comfort, and (3) the memory pathway that contains all your experiences of regained comfort as true solutions have been implemented.*

The first stage in using this technique is to learn how to do self-hypnosis. When I began offering this technique to my patients, I taught them how to do it in my office. We chose a day when the patient could stay longer than the usual session length (forty-five minutes) and when I didn't have another patient immediately following, so that we would have extra time if we needed it. More often than not, we achieved our goal without using the extra time. After trying it at home, my patients often asked for reminders of the directions so I created a written description for them. It then occurred to me that patients might be able, with the written instructions, to learn to do this themselves at home. With subsequent patients, I simply gave them the directions, and they did indeed learn it on their own. They would invariably return with questions. Often they were unsure whether they were doing it correctly because the state feels similar to a normal waking state but, when they described their experience, it was evident that they were achieving self-hypnosis.

You, too, can learn to do this at home. In this and some of the following chapters I will answer many questions that I anticipate you may have. I will first describe the process in detail and then summarize it for easy reference. Do read through the description before you try it because you can't read while you are doing self-hypnosis and you need to arrange a proper environment for yourself.

As you read the following description, you may feel a sense of excitement perhaps mixed with the anticipatory anxiety that one feels when attempting something new. That is to be expected. If, however, your feeling is predominantly a sense of fear or dread you should not attempt self-hypnosis outside the context of a therapeutic situation or without the approval of your psychotherapist.

STAGE 1: ENTERING THE SELF-HYPNOTIC STATE

There are many ways of entering a self-hypnotic state. I have found that the simple method explained below works well. It is adapted from the "Manual for Self-Hypnosis" that I referred to in chapter 1. One stares at a spot on the wall with the expectation that, at some point, the eyes will spontaneously close.

Choose a time when you don't anticipate interruptions. If your time window is limited, set an alarm clock or minute minder for the amount of time you have available. Then you will know when your available time has elapsed and you won't have to think about it. When possible, it is preferable to have an open-ended time span, but it is not essential. When you first begin to do self-hypnosis it may last from a few to about forty-five minutes depending on the quantity and intensity of other stimuli impinging on your mind.

Sit in a comfortable chair in a room where you are alone and don't anticipate being interrupted. Don't lie down because you may go to sleep in that position. Don't cross your legs or fold your hands together because you want to minimize physical sensations. The most comfortable position is usually with the hands on the thighs.

Think for a moment about what the Inner Guide is: a pathway that consists of a sense of its own identity, the wish to help you attain emotional comfort, and the memory pathway that contains all your experiences of regained comfort as true solutions have been implemented. If you wish, you can write this definition on a piece of paper and read it before placing your hands on your thighs. The fact that you wish to have an Inner Guide has caused the mind to form it. It already exists.

Choose a small spot high up on the wall, as high as possible without being uncomfortable to look at. Don't tip your head up, just raise your eyes. It is easier if you can find a real spot; otherwise, choose an imaginary one or make one. Focus your attention on the spot. If you hear noises, disregard them. Remind yourself that they are irrelevant. If an external stimulus occurs that needs to be attended to, such as a telephone call or an itch, take care of it and then resume self-hypnosis. Clear your mind of other thoughts and, as much as possible, think only of the spot. You can think about its color, its size, and its shape, but think only of the spot. After a period of time, the appearance of the spot may change in some way. A bright spot may appear beside it, or a bright halo around it. This is simply an afterimage. It is not necessary to see the spot change, however, in order to enter self-hypnosis.

After a period of time, your eyes will spontaneously feel like closing. When this happens just let them close. At this moment you have entered the self-hypnotic state. The Inner Guide has become dominant. You will probably experience a relaxation of body musculature, manifested by your head tilting forward or your body drooping. You may gently raise your head or body back up if you wish. Gently, in order to minimize the external stimulation caused by your movement. The reason that your body relaxes is because the Inner Guide is a very relaxed, peaceful being. It is now dominant and controls the body. You needn't worry that you have lost control of your body; you haven't. You have voluntarily and temporarily relinquished control to the Inner Guide and you can regain control any time you want to simply by wishing to (not by thinking or wondering about it, but by actually wishing to). That wish serves as a stimulus for which the best response is provided by you rather than by the Inner Guide.

When your eyes have closed, say to yourself that you want your Inner Guide to grow and strengthen. Technically, you want your Inner Guide to repetitively choose true solutions while feeling itself to be real, but the simpler statement suffices. Say this only once. If you repeat it, you are creating an unnecessary and interfering stimulus. When you say it once, you have activated your Inner Guide. It is like calling someone's name to get his attention.

At this point, when you no longer have to focus on the spot, you will find that your mind resumes experiencing its usual thoughts and feelings. You are then free to either let your mind wander or to focus on whatever train of thought you wish. The only subjective difference between the self-hypnotic state and your usual state is that you may feel unusually relaxed. Some of my patients comment on how wonderful it is to feel so relaxed and they look forward to self-hypnosis for that reason alone. Do remember, however, that the feeling of relaxation is incidental; it is not the primary reason for doing self-hypnosis.

You may find that, as you maintain a relaxed state, your eyes periodically open for a moment or even for a while. This occurs when the Inner Guide wishes to provide itself with visual stimulation in order to help it maintain its dominance. When your eyes feel like re-closing, just let them close.

You may or may not experience a loss of awareness that seems similar to sleep. If you do, you will "come to" with a feeling that is slightly different from the feeling of waking. "Coming to" is experienced with a slight jerk or inner reverberation as you regain awareness. It will occur spontaneously if you have entered the self-hypnotic state with an open-ended time frame. It will occur when the necessity for you to resume your usual activities provides a stronger stimulus than the stimuli that the Inner Guide has been responding to. The work of the Inner Guide is equally effective whether or not you experience a loss of awareness. If you do, it is because the current thoughts and feelings in your mind are not sufficient for you to retain your awareness for the full duration of the self-hypnotic session.

When the self-hypnotic state is over, your eyes will open and stay open. You may feel a slight tingling in your hands or feet. Simply move them for a few moments until the tingling disappears. You may feel a continuation of the relaxation, but as you get up and resume your activities, it will dissipate.

To summarize:

(1) Choose a time and place where you don't expect to be interrupted.

(2) Sit in a comfortable chair with your hands on your thighs.

(3) Think for a moment about what the Inner Guide is, and think the thought, "I want my Inner Guide to grow and strengthen."

(4) Focus on a spot high up on the wall. Think only of the spot.

(5) At some point, your eyes will spontaneously close.

(6) You may then let your mind wander.

(7) When the self-hypnotic state is over, your eyes will open.

When, after trying self-hypnosis at home, my patients return with questions, their most common concern is that they aren't doing it properly. They say that they don't feel any differently, just a little relaxed, and that they just keep on thinking as they always do. But this is exactly how one does feel during self-hypnosis. My patients imagine that nothing special can be happening because they are just thinking. But the Inner Guide has become dominant and is in the process of repetitively choosing true solutions for the individual's disequilibrations.

It is accurate to think of the Inner Guide as a friend who is working on your behalf because it does have its own sense of identity, a mind of its own, and it is motivated to help you. That is its purpose. When it first comes into being as a result of your having wished for it, it immediately begins matching disturbances to true solutions. Until self-hypnosis allows it to feel increasingly real, however, it is powerless to help you become aware of and implement these true solutions.

If you have already done meditation of one kind or another, you may find that you have a tendency to revert to your previous technique, either through habit or through desire. You may find that you want to continue using your previous technique and eliciting the content you have previously developed, such as an inner sense of peace, a spiritual presence, or an internal sense of wisdom. You can combine that with self-hypnosis. If you enter the self-hypnotic state as I have described, including the thought that you want your Inner Guide to grow and strengthen, you may then summon up whatever else you want to. Your Inner Guide will be working in its own pathway.

EXTRA ASSISTANCE

I have found that a few people have difficulty doing self-hypnosis because they are unable to focus on the spot. Their mind flits from thought to thought and cannot focus on any one thing for very long, not only during their attempt at self-hypnosis, but much of the time. This has become one of their partial solutions for dealing with inner distress. If your mind works this way, you will need to use an alternate method of focusing. Instead of attempting to focus on a spot, choose the activity you most enjoy and practice imagining that you are doing it. It may be playing a sport, listening to a particular symphony, planning a vacation, or even working. Whatever it is, when you sit as you would for self-hypnosis, think about this favorite activity rather than the spot. Try to daydream that you are actually doing it. In time, you should find that, as you do this, your eyes spontaneously close and you enter the self-hypnotic state. As your distress lessens, you will become able to maintain your focus on whatever you wish to.

A few of my patients were unable to enter the self-hypnotic state because they could not relinquish control to the Inner Guide. They had developed a partial solution of attempting to control everything, like Ben in chapter 3. Thus, they were ambivalent about doing self-hypnosis; they wanted to but they didn't. Although I was not successful in helping them, I have since realized that there may be a way for such people to over-come this problem if they do want to use this technique. It may be possible for them to do self-hypnosis if they are able to main-tain control in some way. They could strike a bargain with the Inner Guide who, if they have wished for one, will already have come into existence. They could state that they would allow it to become dominant for one minute only. They might further stipulate that it not cause their body to relax. The Inner Guide would comply with this because it wants to be helpful. After this initial step had been achieved, they might direct the Inner Guide to become dominant for a slightly longer period of time and they might tell it exactly what they would wish for it to do (if anything) in terms of bodily movement. They might also tell it exactly which problem they would like for it to work on rather than allowing it to decide. In this way, they could main-tain some control over its development. As it worked to decrease their distress, their need for control would gradually ease.

If you are a person for whom control has become a habit

pattern, you may or may not realize it. If you are ambivalent about doing self-hypnosis but would like to give it a try or if you find that you don't go into self-hypnosis, you may turn to this alternate method. Remember, though, that the great majority of people do not have this habit pattern. If you feel that you aren't succeeding at self-hypnosis, it's likely that you are but don't realize it. Remember that in the self-hypnotic state you will feel only a sense of relaxation and will continue thinking your usual thoughts.

STAGE 2: ESTABLISHING A ROUTINE

After you have learned how to enter the self-hypnotic state, the next stage is to establish a way of doing it regularly. Ideally, it should be done every day but for many this is not feasible. You should not try to squeeze it in on a day during which you are too busy because the demands on your time will serve as external stimuli that will interfere. Your attempt will not succeed; it will just be a waste of time. You should, however, try to do it as many days of the week as are comfortably possible. You may feel that you are too busy to do it regularly but those of my patients who are extremely busy have nevertheless found time for it. Decide on a specific time during the day or evening that you feel would be best. Your choice is not written in stone. You can try it and if it doesn't work well you can choose a different time. It is possible to do it at different times on different days but having a regular time will be very helpful in establishing and maintaining the habit.

You may also experiment with the location. If you live alone, you may have a variety of choices. If you live with others, you may choose to tell them what you are doing and why you need to be left alone during that time. Some of my patients find that family members tend initially to walk in on them anyway, out of curiosity. Repeated requests to be left alone are usually effective in ending this disturbance. In some instances, other family members are very interested, and wish to try the technique themselves. If you would prefer not to tell your family, or whoever might be around when you want to do self-hypnosis, you can still find a time and place that will work for you. Some of my patients have found it possible to do it during their lunch hour or other break at work, on certain types of public transportation, early in the morning before others are up, or in the evening when children are asleep and spouses busy with their own activities. With practice, you will be able to enter the self-hypnotic state easily and almost instantaneously.

The time that you spend doing self-hypnosis does not necessarily have to be otherwise unproductive. While your Inner Guide is dominant, you can think about whatever you choose. You may contemplate problems at work and even come up with solutions for them. You may plan for future activities. Or, you may just sink into a pleasant daydream. If these mental activities become insufficiently stimulating, you will lose awareness until the session comes to an end.

Once you have established a routine and are doing self-hypnosis regularly, you will probably find that you are not immediately experiencing any desired changes. You must be patient. At this point, and from here on, the most difficult thing for you to do will be to persist in the absence of immediate reward. Later, I will have some suggestions as to how you can do that. The Inner Guide will be busily at work during all of your waking hours but most efficiently during self-hypnosis, repetitively directing your mind to choose true solutions for your problems. As new, more comfortable ways of handling problems enter awareness, you may find that the Inner Guide is solving problems in a different order than you would have expected. Be patient. The Inner Guide will get to all of your problems in due course. The more conscientious you are about doing self-hypnosis, the sooner you will get results.

STAGE 3: ESTABLISHING COMMUNICATION

Not only will the Inner Guide find true solutions for the anxieties and problems that you know you want help with, it will also find true solutions for problems that you aren't aware of. But in addition to that, it may communicate directly with you, helping you by answering questions that you ask and offering unsolicited information as well. You will want to develop a means of communication with your Inner Guide, unless that feels too strange. If you are wary of this, the Inner Guide will remain silent, it is respectful of your apprehension. A few of my patients have initially preferred not to receive direct communication from their Inner Guide, but the majority have been eager to converse. Some have been successful; others have been frustrated. If you try to establish communication with your Inner Guide and it does not happen at first or even for quite a while, this is because it is too overstimulating, too exciting, to enter awareness. Only after the overstimulation wanes will communication become possible. It usually takes a minimum of several weeks and more often several months.

Occasionally, a person's Inner Guide may determine that it would be best to work silently for a long time. This choice is made when it will most efficiently allow an unwanted or harmful character trait to change. For instance, Ingrid, a woman with a genetically determined inner instability and who had been very dependent on others because of it, hated this need and longed to be independent. Her Inner Guide realized that if it communicated with her, it would represent one more "person" on whom she needed to depend. Instead, it worked silently to strengthen her. When her fragility disappeared she experienced the joy of being independent for the first time. Another example is Jack, a man who was very timid and wanted to depend on others to speak for him. He was able, as his Inner Guide worked silently, to gain confidence and speak for himself. His Inner Guide deliberately remained silent in order to allow him to find his own courage. After this problem had been solved his Inner Guide began communicating with him.

Finger Signals

Communication can occur by means of finger signals, automatic handwriting, inner conversation, or simply having a strong and certain feeling about something. As finger signals may feel less disconcerting than automatic handwriting, it might be best to begin by developing this capability. The Inner Guide can respond to questions that have a yes or no answer by raising a finger. First you must establish which fingers designate which answers. Upon entering the self-hypnotic state, ask the Inner Guide which finger signifies "yes." It is best to ask out loud but in a soft voice. You want to provide that sensory stimulus to the Inner Guide but you don't want to stimulate yourself so intensely through the physical act of vocalization that the self-hypnotic session ends. You may ask several times but if you get no response just continue with the self-hypnotic session as you usually do. You may need to repeat this query for a number of sessions before you get a response. If you don't get a response after a number of sessions, put it off for a while and try again later. At some point, the Inner Guide will respond by causing one of your fingers to rise or, sometimes, merely to tingle. This will be the "yes" finger. Next, ask which finger signifies "no." The Inner Guide will cause a different finger to respond. Finally, ask which finger signifies "I don't know," or "I don't want to say." A third finger will respond. You can then ask the Inner Guide any question that will have a yes or no answer.

Many stimuli are subliminal; they do not enter awareness. The Inner Guide, however, does perceive them, chooses responses, and may tell us about them. For instance, it is possible for the mind to detect whether someone is being honest. If a person is lying, he will either feel a tension that we can perceive out of awareness or, if he is sociopathic, he will have a lack of emotional connection with others that we can also pick up subliminally. You could ask your Inner Guide, "Was so-and-so being honest with me?"

Our minds also register many changes in the physical environment subliminally. You could ask, "Is anyone lurking in this parking lot?" Once you learn how to use finger signals, you can use them anywhere. When you become adept at this you can simply sit or stand in a relaxed position and ask the question without going through a more elaborate entry into the self-hypnotic state.

Our minds register what is going on in our body subliminally and the Inner Guide is aware of those changes. You could ask, if feeling a momentary soreness in the throat, "Am I coming down with a cold?" If feeling a pain in the abdomen, "Do I need to call the doctor?" Or, if performing a new exercise during your workout, "Will I strain a muscle if I continue?"

You may ask about anything that you want to know, anything that you are unsure about. You can ask about relationships and interactions with other people: "Does he really care about me?" "Does she think well of me?" "Is he losing interest in me?" "Did she hurt my feelings deliberately?" "Does he realize he's patronizing me?" "Does she mean what she's saying?" "Was he offended by my remark?"

Or about your work: "Should I change jobs?" "Do I have a chance to get promoted this year?" "Is there a better way to do this?" "Would it be all right for me to leave early today?" "Am I being overly conscientious?"

Or about your life situation: "Would it be a good idea for me to move?" "Should I get the most expensive seats?" "Can I afford to retire?" "Should I make the effort to finish all these errands today?"

Or about your children: "Should I have been more firm with him?" "Was I overly controlling?" "Does she have too many activities?"

More often than not the Inner Guide knows the answers to such questions but occasionally it doesn't have enough information to make a judgment. When it knows the answer it may respond to your question but at times it will choose not to. This may happen for a variety of reasons, which will be discussed later.

I have found that, even though my patients have been told

about the potential for this kind of communication, they never-theless often forget that they can ask about these things. When reminded, they again express surprise that their Inner Guide might be able to answer such questions. It takes time for one to realize the possibilities of this kind of communication.

Also, people who are just beginning to get to know their Inner Guides don't know whether they can trust them. This is normal and healthy. Your Inner Guide will have to prove itself to you. But you will have to give it chances to do so. As you choose to follow its advice, you will come to see that it is right.

Automatic Handwriting

Although the establishment of finger signals will allow you to ask yes or no questions, communication can be expanded by the use of automatic handwriting. Not only can your Inner Guide answer more complex questions, there may be times when it will wish to initiate a conversation. At such times, you will feel moved to get a pencil and paper.

You can ask your Inner Guide by means of finger signals whether it is ready to write. If the answer is "yes," sit in a com-fortable position at a desk or table with a pencil and paper. Hold the pencil to the paper with your arms well supported and enter the self-hypnotic state. You may then gently open your eyes so that your Inner Guide will be able to see what it is doing. Your hand will move of its own accord. At first, the Inner Guide may make just a few squiggles. With practice, it will learn to write. The length of time it takes to begin to write coherently will depend on how disconcerting it is for you to have this happen.

A few of my patients have found that, at least so far, the Inner Guide has done its work silently. Positive changes have occurred but it still hasn't communicated directly. If this is to be your experience, it will happen either because the prospect of direct communication will remain too disequilibrating for a long period of time or because the Inner Guide has a specific reason for remaining silent, as with Ingrid and Jack. Don't be concerned. The Inner Guide will be helping you, progress will occur, and communication will come in time.

When your Inner Guide becomes able to write to you, it may convey more and different information than you expect. It may inform you of things that you didn't think to ask about. For instance, it may choose to tell you about certain characteristics of someone in your life. It may suggest that you make certain purchases. Or it may give you hints about how your life will change. As you receive this information and realize its value you will become more convinced of the Inner Guide's reality and of its capacity to help you.

Inner Thought

At some point you may discover that if you ask the Inner Guide a question, it will answer you by means of inner thought. You may have conversations with it. And, as with handwriting, it may choose to speak to you when you aren't expecting it. I remember one of the first things my Inner Guide said to me. As I was talking with someone, it said, "She's lying." For some people, inner conversation occurs before they have established finger signals or automatic handwriting.

Sometimes your Inner Guide's communication may be made known to you simply by your experiencing a powerful feeling about something and a feeling of sureness about that feeling. If you want corroboration you may ask for it by means of finger signals or handwriting.

Sometimes during inner thought conversations you may wonder, "Was that my Inner Guide speaking; or was it just me, because I want this answer?" At such times, too, you may ask for corroboration by finger signals or handwriting. They can be more convincing than inner thought because they provide a physical sensation of spontaneous movement.

Other Forms of Communication

Your Inner Guide may occasionally communicate with you non-verbally by presenting a mental image, causing you to move in a particular way, or causing you to position objects in particular configurations. For instance, my Inner Guide led me to hang some pictures on the wall in a specific pattern. The Inner Guides of some people I know have communicated with me through visual cues. One instance occurred when a visiting friend absent-mindedly fiddled with some objects on a table, subtly rearranging them. After she left, I noticed that they now formed a pattern. A bud vase containing a lovely flower was now surrounded by several pencils, their ends all pointing inward to call attention to it. I stared at it, wondering what it meant. My Inner Guide helped me understand that her Inner Guide had taken that opportunity to express her gratitude for my help. There are times when an image can be more powerful and effective than words.

STAGE 4: TRUSTING YOUR INNER GUIDE

Once you establish communication by means of handwriting or inner thought, you may ask your Inner Guide for its name. It will choose a name for itself that it may reveal to you. It may also choose to give you an image of itself, through inner visualization (an image in the mind's eye). It is useful for the Inner Guide to have a name. That will help it to feel more real, which will increase the power with which it can work to solve your problems and ameliorate your discomforts. It may choose a name for a specific purpose, to help you think about yourself in a new way, but most often the name it chooses is one that represents your ideal self. Those of my patients who have learned their Inner Guide's names have been surprised by the choice, but then have understood why it was chosen. Some have at first, and sometimes for a long time, felt skeptical about whether such a wonderful being, an ideal self, could possibly be an active part of them. All of us who have had this experience so far have grasped only slowly what a benign, peaceful, knowledgeable, powerful, helpful friend we have developed. As you gradually realize this, you learn that you can absolutely rely on your Inner Guide's judgment and its power to help you.

Speedreading

There is one other thing you can do to hasten and further your progress. Your Inner Guide can act only on the information in your memory. There may be areas of information that you have never been exposed to or for which your knowledge is incomplete. You may not have learned all that would be useful to know about your body or about the world around you. You can correct this by reading, but rather than reading in the usual way you can look at each page for just a moment. I call this "speedreading." In so doing, you will have registered the information in your memory. You will not have access to it but your Inner Guide will. Of course, you can always slow down and read for your own comprehension too when you want to.

Your Inner Guide will use this knowledge as it searches for true solutions to your problems. Remember my experience when I got caught in the traffic jam: my Inner Guide consulted the map of the city that was in my memory and got me back to the office on time. Inner Guides don't provide this kind of information just for your interest or curiosity but they will use it when they feel that it is necessary. Reading materials should be chosen carefully as they vary in quality. One way to learn about a specific subject would be to look in a college bookstore at the assigned reading list for courses in that area.

STAGE 5: COMPLETION

Once you have come to completely trust your Inner Guide you will feel much more relaxed, knowing that it is working silently to fully resolve all remaining problems. As it does so, it inflluences you to think, feel, and act in ways that will bring you the greatest comfort and happiness. When all past problems have been resolved, it will handle all new disequilibrations efficiently and maintain an optimal stimulus level.

* * *

As you can see, this process takes time. The most difficult thing for you to do is to persevere in the absence of immediate results. I have found that progress occurs most rapidly for those of my patients who have been conscientious in doing self-hypnosis. For those of you whose problems are greater, it will take longer for your Inner Guide to complete the work but you will experience improvement and increasing comfort all along the way.

You are now ready to begin the adventure. The next chapters describe what you can expect to experience along the way.

CHAPTER 7

WHAT WILL YOUR EXPERIENCE BE?

THE INNER GUIDE, from the moment of its formation, seeks true solutions for all discomforts. For some disturbances true solutions are available, such as the knowledge that we can eat when we are hungry if food is available. For other disturbances we must rely on partial solutions, such as waiting for the next meal when food is not immediately available. Often, however, partial solutions that are initially useful later become maladaptive.

I have already described the example of the lonely woman who eats too much because she has come to equate food with love. Most of us experienced a linkage of food with love during infancy as we were provided with food by a loving caretaker. This is one reason why we find food so pleasurable. During this woman's development, however, she experienced significant loneliness for which eating represented the partial solution that brought the greatest relief. Eating then became locked in as her response. Later, as other possibilities became available she wasn't able to make use of them. If she develops her Inner Guide, however, it will find the true solution for her loneliness; namely, finding someone to share her life with. She can then forgo excessive eating because it will not lead to the result she wishes.

Typically, partial solutions that have become maladaptive have originated as responses to the major disturbances of early life: physical discomforts and traumas, fears of abandonment and other dangers, and intense feelings such as anger, sadness, and even love. For most if not all of these problems true solutions will later be available.

As the Inner Guide now identifies these solutions we are not aware of its activity because it does this work silently. We will, however, be aware of its subsequent actions!

COMPLEX STIMULI

Once a true solution has been identified, an interruption must occur in the previous habit pattern in order for the mind to choose the new solution. Although such interruptions may occur by chance from time to time, the Inner Guide can cause them to occur. We no longer need to wait for spontaneously occurring interruptions. As her Inner Guide causes the lonely woman to forget a fork when setting the table (as described in chapter 5), she is confronted with a contradiction when she sits down to eat. The incomplete place setting simultaneously signifies that she can eat and that she can't. The resulting pause allows her mind to select the new, true solution.

In psychoanalysis or psychoanalytically-oriented psychotherapy, the therapeutic situation itself provides the necessary interruptions. As a patient develops transferences toward the therapist, the therapist becomes a complex stimulus because he or she is experienced as a transference object and a real object simultaneously. Henry (described in chapter 4) developed a transference to his therapist. He fell in love with her, experiencing her as though she were his mother. But, simultaneously, he was aware that she was not. She provided him with a true solution with the interpretation that a part of him was experiencing her as he had his mother when he was young but that, although she was not his mother and not available to him, he is now able as an adult to find a woman in his current life to love. Because she served as a complex stimulus, it was possible for the true solution to replace the previous maladaptive one.

While the treatment situation provides the therapist as a built-in complex stimulus allowing maladaptive solutions to be replaced by true solutions systematically, the Inner Guide does so by causing complex stimuli to occur at relevant moments. Forgetting a fork is one example.

What sorts of things will your Inner Guide do to create complex stimuli for you? It may cause you to drop things, spill things, forget things, misplace things, make slips of the tongue, or take a left instead of a right when driving. However, it will never do anything that causes a serious problem. The things that you drop are not breakable, the things that you spill don't cause stains, the things that you forget are remembered later, the things that you misplace always turn up, your slips of the tongue are never hurtful to others, and you won't take a wrong turn if it would result in your having to go far out of your way or be late for something important.

The Inner Guide may sometimes decline to answer questions that you ask. Instead of raising the "yes" or "no" fingers, it may raise both. Or, while writing, it may choose to scribble, or begin to give an answer and then stop.

You might find yourself habitually repeating an act, such as double-checking to see whether you have turned out a light or re-checking your schedule for the next day. While some people repeat actions as part of an obsessive-compulsive disorder, your repetitions will be caused by your Inner Guide as one more way to create complex stimuli. When you feel compelled to repeat an act rather than proceed with your chosen activity, you again experience a contradiction: you are moved to proceed but simultaneously moved to repeat.

The Inner Guide may also cause you to sustain very minor

injuries from time to time. Don't worry. The Inner Guide won't do this to you if it would be too upsetting for you. It doesn't want to increase your distress. An injury makes an excellent complex stimulus because each time you attempt to do something that hurts and then stop, you are experiencing a contradiction: you simultaneously intend to do something, but you can't. For instance, if the Inner Guide causes you to stub your toe, you may find as you walk up stairs that you want to position that foot differently so that your toe doesn't hurt. Each time you forget to reposition your foot and feel the pain, you will experience a complex stimulus: you can take a step; you can't. Many instances of a complex stimulus may therefore occur as a result of one action of the Inner Guide. (Inner Guides are very efficient.)

Even the delay in becoming aware of a new solution due to the need for its repetition causes uncertainty. We are kept in suspense regarding when the changes we hope for will occur: "Maybe it will happen this month; maybe it won't. I can plan on it; I can't." Anything that causes uncertainty will form a complex stimulus.

What you experience will depend on your current level of distress. If you are too busy and typically feel rushed, if you are depressed and feel depleted, or if you have a very difficult work or home situation, you are already very disequilibrated. Your Inner Guide will not aggravate the situation by causing you to experience time-consuming mistakes such as misplacing or forgetting things, or annoying actions such as dropping things or taking wrong turns. It may just give you some "yes" and "no" answers simultaneously, or sometimes scribble instead of writing. Or, if even these minimally frustrating things feel too upsetting, it may simply rely on the complex stimuli that occur naturally as a result of your distress. For example, if you are rushing to an appointment and fear you might be late, the resulting uncertainty can provide an interruption of the habit of pushing yourself too hard. If you are unsure whether you will ever feel less depressed, that ambiguity can serve to interrupt the partial solution of depression. If you are in doubt about an externally generated problem, such as the possibility of losing your job, that uncertainty can furnish an interruption of a maladaptive reaction to this situation such as denial of the problem, or procrastination in dealing with it.

A major life change, whether positive (marriage, parenthood, promotion, special achievement) or negative (illness or injury, loss of a loved one or a position) provides a special opportunity for change. These events are the source of many complex stimuli, because they interrupt routine and cause one to do many things differently. If you experience such an event, your Inner Guide will take advantage of the many naturally occurring complex stimuli that will result.

If naturally occurring moments of uncertainty can interrupt habit patterns, why does the Inner Guide often cause instances of minor mischief in addition? The more interruptions we experience, the sooner these habit patterns will be altered. Some of my patients who have initially been spared the deliberate interruptions because their situations have been so difficult, have found that, as they have improved and become somewhat less distressed their Inner Guides have begun to cause various minor mishaps. How frequently might these occur? Perhaps several times during a day, but often none for weeks at a time. Your Inner Guide will determine what you can tolerate without becoming overly disturbed. As you come to understand the usefulness of these moments, you will become tolerant and even accepting of them. Sometimes you may even be amused by them.

When a minor mishap occurs, you probably won't understand why it has been chosen because you won't be aware of the habit pattern that is being interrupted. For instance, Amanda (described in chapter 3) takes care of others at her own expense. If she were to develop an Inner Guide, it might cause her to drop something she is fetching for her husband or take a wrong turn on the way to a needy friend's house. She won't understand why she is making these mistakes as long as she has not yet understood that she is doing too much for others. If she were to ask her Inner Guide whether it has caused these errors and if so why, it might choose to tell her.

You also won't initially understand why your Inner Guide might give you a "yes" and a "no" signal simultaneously. This complex stimulus can interrupt a habit pattern that is expressed in a question that you are unaware is problematic. For instance, Amanda might ask whether she should take a dinner dish to her bedridden acquaintance before or after she makes dinner for her husband. She would be unaware that taking food to this person is beyond what she can reasonably expect herself to do. Her Inner Guide might give her a "yes" and "no" complex stimulus to interrupt the habit of feeding her acquaintances. Or it might cause her to double-check her oven or nick her finger with her paring knife. Is it really worth it for her to cut her finger? Yes, if necessary. Think of the relief she will feel when she can relax and stop rushing to help everyone else. It will be a profound change for her. Actually, because her life is so hectic she is one of those for whom the Inner Guide would initially rely on naturally occurring complex stimuli. It would only introduce deliberate mishaps when she has already made some progress toward achieving comfort.

How is it helpful to be kept in suspense regarding when a change that you wish for will occur? The uncertainty creates a complex stimulus that can interrupt a wish that stems from a harmful habit pattern. For example, Amanda might wish that her Inner Guide would find a way for her to fit in even more acts of helpfulness and she would wonder how and when this might occur. Could she plan on volunteering at the hospital next month? Or not until the following month? Should she try to change her schedule now? She should, yet perhaps she shouldn't. This complex stimulus will allow a new solution to be chosen: namely, that she should decrease her activities rather than increase them.

REPETITION

Once the Inner Guide has identified a true solution and has caused or taken advantage of a complex stimulus to replace the previous maladaptive solution with the new one, a third step is necessary. The true solution must be repeated until its novelty wanes so that it is no longer too over-stimulating to enter awareness. Only then can it be implemented.

Repetition of the new solution occurs whenever the mind is stimulated by the problem. The Inner Guide can increase the frequency of the repetition by causing more stimulation. It can do this by causing more minor mishaps because they have become associatively related to the stimulus. For instance, the lonely woman who eats too much will forget her fork not once, but a number of times. Another way that repetition is increased is through self-hypnosis because when the Inner Guide becomes dominant it experiences sensations. Thus, it experiences each stimulus more intensely, prolonging the reverberation of the response. This is why it is so important for you to do self-hypnosis regularly.

Yet another way for the Inner Guide to increase repetition of the new solution is by increasing exposure to the problem. This may seem paradoxical, as the Inner Guide's wish is to solve the problem, but repetition of the problem will, in fact, hasten awareness and implementation. For example, Amanda's Inner Guide might cause her to think of new ways to help people. She won't be able to follow through with them because she won't have time but the thoughts will result in repetition of the new solution (that she should do less, not more).

Sometimes, when a true solution has been locked into a stimulus but before it comes into awareness, the overstimulation caused by the change is so intense that the mind may discharge some of the excitement by causing bodily movement: by drumming the fingers or tapping the feet. Or, insomnia may occur. This sleeplessness differs from that caused by worry. One feels keyed up rather than distressed. You may at first not realize that these experiences are caused by excitement rather than anxiety.

At times the intense work that is going on out of awareness may cause a feeling of fatigue. But do remember that the Inner Guide doesn't want to cause distress and will balance the desire to achieve emotional comfort with the necessity to live, function, and have pleasure in the present.

True solutions for disturbances often consist of the knowledge that one no longer has to do certain things or feel certain painful emotions. When Amanda was a child her legitimate desires were criticized by her mother who considered them selfish. It was for this reason that she developed the habit pattern of helping others at her own expense. It decreased her feeling of guilt but prevented her from fulfilling her own desires and, as it grew, it came to consume her time and attention. For her, a true solution is the knowledge that her mother was wrong, that she need not feel guilty and that she can relinquish this habit. With the help of her Inner Guide, she will gradually stop taking care of others at her own expense and will no longer feel "stressed out." She will feel relieved and liberated.

In Amanda's case, the misguided habit pattern was a response that was closely related, associatively, to the problem. She took unselfishness to an extreme as a response to accusations of selfishness. In others, however, a habit pattern of busily helping others might serve simply as a distraction from an unrelated disturbance or as a tension-reducing mechanism. In such instances, the habit pattern will cease when the level of disturbance has diminished.

Most people have developed a repertoire of partial solutions that serve either as distractions or as discharges of tension. Examples of such activities include keeping the radio or television on continuously, talking with other people endlessly, attending too many social events, running unnecessary errands, shopping excessively, accumulating possessions that aren't really needed or enjoyed, planning activities in too much detail, doing other people's work for them, doing things too carefully, engaging in activities which are only of peripheral interest, and so forth. Your repertoire may include some of these activities. They will subside as your level of discomfort diminishes. As they end, you will feel a sense of lightness and peace. You will have more time and more space for yourself.

As this happens, you will be able to refashion your life and your surroundings to increase your pleasure and comfort. While a true solution may result in the cessation of certain habits, it can also initiate different ones. Amanda, when she has learned that her own desires are legitimate, can begin to fulfill them. She can do things for herself. She may choose to buy new clothes, go to concerts, remodel her home, get a better car, or relax in the evening with a good book. Some of these activities will require extra energy. She will find that she has more than enough energy for them because, as her chronic disturbances are solved and disappear, the work that has been required to respond to them with partial solutions is no longer necessary.

She will learn that she needs to take care of herself first. She may then choose to do certain things for others. She will not be compelled to as part of a misguided partial solution but, once having had her own needs and desires fulfilled, she will have something extra within herself to give to others. She will choose what, when, and to whom.

VARIATIONS IN SENSITIVITY

If you are more sensitive than most, you may be unaware that you are. You may assume that others feel the same way that you do. Likewise, if you are easygoing, you may assume that your state is the natural one and view sensitive people as "overreacting" to situations.

If you are highly sensitive, you can feel pleasures very intensely and can easily appreciate subtleties and complexities. However, you will be more distressed by a wide variety of unpleasant stimuli: physical, cognitive, and emotional. Because of this, your mind will choose false solutions more often. Pathways that, out of awareness, experience the stimuli full force will be stored in the memory, forming a reservoir of distress. When new stimuli occur that are associatively related they will evoke the stored distress, causing you to "overreact." But your Inner Guide, by integrating split-off pathways, will cause the heightened response to distressful stimuli to end and the reservoir of distress to be emptied. It will also help you handle or avoid noxious stimuli.

What if you are an easygoing individual? You are spared the discomfort of reacting to unpleasant stimuli as strongly as a sensitive person and, in fact, your even-tempered nature often helps you feel enjoyably mellow. But are you destined to enjoy pleasure less intensely? No, because as your Inner Guide solves your discomforts, the "static" they cause will dissipate, allowing you to more easily access what were previously subliminal perceptions. This will increase your sensitivity to pleasurable stimuli.

Physical Well-being

Your Inner Guide will help you take good care of yourself and give yourself all that you need. Some disequilibrations stem from physical discomfort. Hunger can be solved by eating well, fatigue by getting enough sleep.

Physical fitness can be achieved and maintained through regular exercise. Pilates, which I described in chapter 1, is one form of exercise that not only maintains physical fitness but provides an additional benefit as well. Because it requires focus on all parts of the body simultaneously, it causes many stimulus-response pathways in the mind to be activated simultaneously. This results in their integration with the development of new pathways that contain all the elements of the previously separate individual pathways. As a result, when any physical movement is initiated, there is reverberation through the entire network of mental pathways relating to movement, which results in heightened muscle tone throughout the body. This contributes to the maintenance of an optimal level of disequilibration in the mind, which brings about a sense of well-being. Any form of vigorous activity releases endorphins that contribute to such a feeling for a period of time but the heightened muscle tone resulting from Pilates is continuous. And, because Pilates requires intense focus on the exercise itself, there is minimal contamination by the distractions of competition or performance that occur with sports or dance.

Because of its access to subliminal stimuli, your Inner Guide can monitor your health. It will notice minimal deviations in your appearance, such as a growing mole or a minute change in skin color. As we become ill or are injured, changes occur in our physiology. Physical traumas and infections cause an inflammatory response. Organ malfunctions result in a deficit of necessary substances and the accumulation of toxins. One of the effects of these physiological changes is a feeling of malaise or vague bodily discomfort.

When an illness is just beginning, the feeling of malaise is subliminal. Only the Inner Guide is aware of it. Knowing that you are acquiring an illness, it can influence you to take special steps to abort or attenuate it. At such times you may find yourself going to bed early, moderating or skipping a physical workout, and avoiding or postponing stressful encounters. If, during these times, you might tend to think of yourself as lazy, know instead that your Inner Guide is intervening in order to keep you well.

Perhaps your illness is one that will progress. Because your Inner Guide has access to all of your past experience, it can draw upon memories of past illnesses and on whatever medical knowledge you have acquired through visits to doctors and reading. Often, this is sufficient for it to diagnose a current illness. Your Inner Guide will know whether you need to see a doctor.

It can also detect the subliminal discomfort resulting from minor injuries that occur during physical exertion and can influence your movement so that subtle guarding occurs, thus preventing exacerbation of those injuries. And it can help you maintain your balance when you otherwise might fall by its exquisite sense of your position in space.

With its capacity for subliminal perception, the Inner Guide can also protect you from various dangers. A slight movement in a dark parking lot, bodily tension in an approaching stranger, a subliminal odor of smoke, all will be detected. You will be influenced to avoid or remove yourself from such situations.

HANDLING UNPLEASANT SITUATIONS

Many disturbances that arise from unpleasant stimuli in your surroundings are all too apparent. While sometimes emanating from physical sources, such as extremes of weather or excessive noise, they most often stem from interactions with other people. Your Inner Guide can provide new solutions to help you avoid, insulate yourself from, or otherwise handle these discomforts. When someone is being unpleasant, your Inner Guide will provide a true solution. Most often, this will involve removing yourself from the situation or giving the other a non-response such as silence or the most minimal comment. This denies reinforcement to the offending person. It also minimizes the disturbance you feel. For example, if another driver cuts you off you will actually remain disturbed longer if you honk in anger than if you don't because your action will cause a longer reverberation in your mind.

Sometimes, the optimal response to another's unpleasantness will be a matter-of-fact confrontation that can be offered quite gently, though firmly. Confrontations are useful when you wish to help people understand that they are being unpleasant. Confrontation may also be necessary to prevent an escalation of unpleasantness. I use the term "confrontation" not in the everyday sense of the word but rather as it is used in my field, as a technical term that means pointing something out or making something evident. Confrontations can be very quiet and even quite indirect. For instance, if someone whom you know to be envious of you asks how you are, hoping or assuming that you aren't doing well, you can reply, "Very well, thank you." That person will be taken aback and will at least subliminally register that the wish had been otherwise.

Your Inner Guide can help you with minor annoyances. When a driver cuts in front of you, when your train is late, when a salesperson is rude to you, when an appliance breaks —all of these situations and many more typically evoke the response of irritation or anger. Anger in response to an annoyance is a habit pattern that is formed early in life. For infants and young children, a feeling and its physical expression is often the only response because they do not yet have the skills and resources to access a better solution. An angry response to one who is perceived as an aggressor or a frustrater, such as a bullying playmate or a limit-setting parent, becomes generalized as a response to any kind of aggression (rude drivers, rude salespeople) or frustration (late trains, broken appliances).

When a driver cuts in front of you or when a salesperson is rude to you, the best possible solution, the true solution, is the knowledge that it doesn't really matter. Yes, the other person was wrong but it's not important. Perhaps you are aware of this, yet you may be unable to turn off your anger. You may not even want to because it has been locked in as a partial solution to the problem and does diminish your distress even if it doesn't end it. You remain upset. Your Inner Guide can resolve this disturbance by creating a complex stimulus, then expediting the new solution's entry into awareness. For example, while attempting to pay for the item sold to you by the rude salesperson, your Inner Guide may cause you to reach into the wrong compartment of your wallet or purse for your credit card. You reach for it and it isn't there! For that instant, you are paying, yet you are not: a complex stimulus. The true solution, that it isn't important, can then become locked in. As your Inner Guide thinks about it repeatedly until its novelty has waned, it will enter awareness.

YOUR WORK

In addition to helping you take good care of yourself and handle unpleasant stimuli, your Inner Guide will help you make your life situation what you want it to be. Perhaps you are unhappy in your work. If you chose your occupation for any reason other than love of the work and the feeling that you could become good at it, you are unfulfilled. Many have drifted into a job because they didn't know what they wanted to do and just accepted the first opportunity that came along. Some were steered into areas that their parents wanted for them. Others were afraid to strike out on their own and gravitated toward situations that provided emotional support. Some wanted to live up to others' expectations or to be like someone they idealized. Quite a few have been attracted by the prospect of prestige or financial rewards. Many are doing much less than they have the potential for, like Dorothy in chapter 3. Although many people know that they don't like their work, many more who are unfulfilled don't realize it. They don't know how much pleasure and satisfaction they could get from work that would be right for them.

Everybody has the capacity to develop a passion, something that they care about deeply. As we develop, we respond with more pleasure to stimuli that evoke our natural talents and capabilities and we seek more stimuli that will repeat those experiences. For instance, a tall and very well-coordinated youngster will get more enjoyment from playing basketball than will others because he gets more pleasurable kinesthetic feedback and more delight from his rapid improvement as he exercises his greater capability. Those who have artistic talent, an easy grasp of mathematical or scientific concepts, a special rapport with other people, or some other special aptitude will get intense pleasure from those activities.

Some have experienced special gratification from certain activities that have solved past problems, not only because these activities have restored comfort but also because they provide a sense of mastery as they develop. Such processes include building things, fixing things, designing things, organizing things, producing things, or planning things.

The content of one's passion is also derived from early pleasures. The fascination of viewing pond water under a microscope, or the moon through a telescope, the enchantment of seeing a play or a ballet, the joy of caressing a doll, the excitement of building a tree house—whatever experiences have provided the most enjoyable level of stimulation and have related most closely to one's capabilities will have the deepest meaning.

Why do so few realize their passion? More often than not, discomforts that result in maladaptive habit patterns interfere. For instance, Amanda is caught up in her need to do things for others. The stimuli for this habit pattern (ingrained feelings of guilt) are so disturbing, as is the habit pattern itself, that they monopolize awareness. When her Inner Guide solves these problems, she will then be able to respond to the disequilibrations caused by her own needs and desires. Only after she has attained some comfort will these disturbances subside sufficiently so that she can become aware of her most authentic, heartfelt interests.

Sometimes a person's passion is so intense that it can be exercised despite misguided habit patterns but it will be contaminated by them. For instance, a musician with significant performance anxiety may play well nevertheless but not as exquisitely as would otherwise be possible. Someone who has a talent for management may run a successful business but if the talent is contaminated by greed or a need to show off, judgment will suffer. In addition, the pleasure of the work will be diluted.

Your Inner Guide, by solving your discomforts, will make it possible for you to work well, effectively, and with pleasure. If your job is not right for you, you will be helped to make a change. If you haven't yet discovered your passion or if it has been compromised by maladaptive habit patterns, the work of your Inner Guide will free it.

YOUR RELATIONSHIPS

Perhaps you are having difficulty with a relationship. What might be complicating it? If your partner or friend is unable to care about you or treat you well and unwilling to try to change or if there is a mismatch of goals or interests, then you will be uncomfortable if you are unable to leave. Your Inner Guide can help you end the relationship or change it to a more casual connection.

What if the problem lies with you? Many misguided habit patterns can interfere with a relationship. A person may be needy, self-centered, controlling, hurtful, masochistic, or inhibited, or may have difficulty being loyal or faithful. One who is significantly anxious or depressed will have difficulty sharing the feeling of closeness with another. Many have a tendency to develop transferences that distort their perceptions. They confuse a person with someone from their past. With a negative transference, they attribute undesirable characteristics to that person. For example, Amanda experiences her husband as critical, as her mother was, and she is afraid of him. With a positive transference, a person will be loved or idealized for characteristics that belong to a past figure. This too is harmful because one can't be empathic with others if one doesn't recognize them for who they are.

The Inner Guide, by exchanging maladaptive habit patterns for true solutions, will make it possible for you to love comfortably and unconditionally those whom you wish to be close to. What is love? It is the feeling that is evoked by a pleasurable stimulus that has been repeated frequently enough to cause an intensely positive response. We can love many things: objects, places, times, processes, ideas, people, food, works of art, the city, the country, sunrise, springtime, reading, writing, freedom, charity, relatives, and friends. Because the greatest potential for varied and repetitive stimulation comes from another human being, it is a person that we can respond to most intensely, love most fully and deeply. We will want to give all we can to such a loved one and the greatest gift we can give is the gift of understanding because, in so doing, we will be meeting our loved one's needs most fully and also experiencing the greatest closeness.

RAISING CHILDREN

If you have children, you may feel uncertain at times about what is best for them. Over the past decades various theories of child rearing have been prevalent at different times and have ranged from the very strict to the very permissive. Each undoubtedly originated as a response to a disequilibrating stimulus. For instance, the past injunction to feed a baby at strict four-hour intervals was an attempt to prevent diarrhea, which was prevalent at that time. Currently, conflicting advice is available and it includes not only the recommendations of various experts but also suggestions to ignore them all! The purpose of any approach, presumably, is to raise an individual who will be competent, of good character and, hopefully, emotionally comfortable. How will your Inner Guide help you with this?

As we know, infants experience many discomforts, some obvious, others mystifying. We do the best we can to maintain their optimal level of comfort as we tend to their physical needs. We attempt to soothe them when they are upset and provide them with stimulation as we interact with them. We must also allow them to experience frustration, in reasonable doses, so that they will develop the capacity to delay gratification without becoming unduly distressed.

The difficulties in knowing what to do for them and when (and what not to do and when) arise from interferences in our empathy due to the mental static generated by our own discomforts. If you are anxious about aspects of your own life, you may be too preoccupied at times to attend to your baby's feelings or, on the other hand, you may overreact if the baby's distress stimulates your own reservoir of anxiety. If you have been frustrated in your own desires you may attempt to fulfill them vicariously through your child but in so doing you will be inflicting noxious intrusions that interfere with optimal development. If you have been deprived yourself or have difficulties with aggression, you may be overly permissive. Then your children will suffer from a lack of needed structure and will have difficulties in understanding boundaries.

Children will identify with the people in their environment who offer the best solutions for discomforts. To the extent that parents are hampered by non-optimal solutions to their own problems, they will, of course, not be able to offer the best example. The parent who wants his child to live out his own ambitions is also failing to set an example of a person who is happily fulfilling his own desires. A parent who is free of maladaptive solutions to problems will set an ideal example for his child.

You can turn to your Inner Guide for the best advice on how to respond to your children. It is fully attuned to their needs and will know how you may best handle the various problems that arise. If your Inner Guide has chosen to work silently for the time being, you may find yourself feeling a strong impetus to respond to your child in a certain way. That impetus may be a manifestation of your Inner Guide.

When you have developed your Inner Guide fully you will be able to live very comfortably and provide the best example for your children. Also, having minimized the mental static that comes from unresolved problems, you will be exquisitely attuned to their needs for gratification, frustration, and protection from excess over- and understimulation. You will also feel the greatest delight in your children's personalities and development!

* * *

Why, Amanda wonders, is her Inner Guide telling her not to help her neighbor? Your Inner Guide will help you do the right thing in any situation. This may not always seem so but the Inner Guide knows best. It has access to all of your memories; hence it has a greater knowledge base with which to make decisions. It is motivated to provide you with maximal comfort.

Occasionally, when you feel more disturbed by someone else's discomfort than by your own, your Inner Guide will lead you to take care of the other's problem. For instance, a parent will get up in the middle of the night to take care of a baby in distress.

Anger will be felt only in response to true provocation and will subside quickly because you will handle the cause expeditiously. Feelings of sadness will be felt only for real losses, not for imaginary or transferential ones. Feelings of guilt will disappear altogether. Guilt is a pathological emotion. It is a response to one's impression that one has done something wrong. With the Inner Guide's help, you will do what is right. Because you will fulfill your potential and become your ideal self, you will have no reason to feel shame.

All of these changes will occur gradually. As you know, they can only occur when the Inner Guide has had the opportunity to identify true solutions, provide complex stimuli so that the new solutions can replace the previous ones, and cause sufficient repetition so that the true solutions may reach awareness and be implemented. More often than not, one recognizes these changes only in retrospect.

Amanda will think, "Hm, I don't seem to be so busy anymore." The Inner Guide may not solve problems in the order you wish for because the greatest changes will require the most repetition in order to reach awareness and be implemented. Over time, all maladaptive habit patterns will be replaced. Because your own needs will be met so well, you will have much to give to others and that will give you great pleasure.

CHAPTER 8

RESULTS

I HAVE DESCRIBED the kinds of changes that you can expect if you do self-hypnosis conscientiously. What have others experienced? Here are some examples.

Kay resolved every year on New Year's Day to lose the extra weight she carried. She had learned as an infant, as we all have, to associate food with being loved and soothed. But her self-absorbed mother was frequently out of touch with Kay's anxiety and her need for comforting and reassurance. Kay's mind matched the stimulus of anxiety with the solution of eating to soothe herself, and this became locked in as a habit pattern.

In her teens she went on short-lived crash diets and as an adult she tried various dieting plans that ranged from sensible to extreme. Regardless of the method, she invariably reverted to her habit pattern and failed to achieve her goal. She was well aware that her weight was bad for her health and blamed herself for her inability to stick to a diet. Why was she able to lose some weight at the beginning of a new program, only to gain it back? Each time that her distress at being overweight became the greatest source of discomfort, she began a diet. But other sources of anxiety: worries about her job, her apartment, or her finances would quickly supervene. Her locked-in response to all of these problems was to eat. It had been an adaptive response when she was very young because she didn't yet have other solutions. As she grew and gained autonomy better choices, which are true solutions, became possible but were out of reach.

When she began doing self-hypnosis, she continued her previous pattern for quite some time. Why didn't her Inner Guide intervene to help her stay on her diet? Her Inner Guide had other priorities. Because Kay's mother had emotionally abandoned her, she also suffered from ongoing depression that she didn't recognize as a problem because she was so accustomed to it. The depression was, in fact, a greater problem than her weight because it affected every aspect of her life including her ability to stay on a diet. Her Inner Guide's first priority was to attend to that problem. After Kay's depression had receded, her Inner Guide addressed the weight problem and Kay became able to diet effectively. She developed a well-balanced meal plan with a caloric level that allowed her to lose weight slowly and steadily.

* * *

Linda, a married woman, came for treatment because she had begun to engage in brief sexual encounters with other men whom she didn't particularly care for or respect. Following each incident she would chastise herself and wonder why she would behave in a way that felt so out of character. Having some knowledge of psychology, she wondered whether she was acting out some sort of Oedipal fantasy.

She was interested in trying self-hypnosis and, after her Inner Guide had developed, it explained to her that she had engaged in these encounters to try to prove to herself that she was unaffected by sex (a false solution). When she was a young girl, she had been sexually molested by a friend of her father on several occasions. She dimly recalled this but had no memory of any feeling about it. Her Inner Guide told her that she had been very frightened and was horrified that she had been "dirtied." If that were the case, she asked, why hadn't she turned to her parents for help? Her Inner Guide explained that the man had told her that she had done something very bad and shouldn't tell anyone or she would be punished. Her feelings had been buried, out of awareness, because they were so distressing.

But why, she wondered, did she begin having these sexual encounters now? She then recalled that some time ago she had seen a movie about sexual abuse. It had been very graphic and she had felt uncomfortable as she watched it. She wanted to walk out but didn't want to be conspicuous. Did that movie jog the buried memories? Her Inner Guide told her that it had indeed, and that her previous solution of "forgetting" had to be augmented by additional solutions. She needed to feel as though sex couldn't affect her.

Linda wondered whether she should confront her abuser, now an elderly man. Would that help her overcome this trauma? Her Inner Guide explained that this would be harmful because it would intensify the stimulus of the memory and cause it to become associated with additional related stimuli. This would prolong her discomfort and increase the work that her Inner Guide would need to do in order to end it. As Linda understood the cause of her sexual encounters, they ceased and she began for the first time to experience sexual pleasure with her husband. She hadn't previously realized that she had been frigid. That knowledge, too, had been kept out of awareness.

How did these changes occur? The memory of the abuse had been matched to the false solutions of amnesia and frigidity and, when strongly evoked by the movie, matched also to the false solution that Linda could not be affected by sex with an inappropriate man. She needed to have the sexual encounters in order to prove that she was not affected. Her Inner Guide accessed the true solution, that she had indeed been affected but that this experience was now a thing of the past. It then caused a relevant complex stimulus to occur, allowing the memory to be linked with the new solution. During self-hypnosis her Inner Guide repetitively thought about the new solution until its novelty waned sufficiently to enter Linda's awareness.

* * *

Martha found herself becoming increasingly angry. At work, her efforts were not rewarded by her boss. Some of her co-workers, who were less experienced than she was, were promoted over her. It appeared that they advanced by currying favor with the boss. Martha felt trapped because in the current economic climate there were no other job openings in her city and she did not want to leave the area. Her mood had become one of almost constant dull anger and she began having frequent headaches. She reacted strongly to minor annoyances and drove so aggressively that she became afraid that she might cause an accident. Her anger at her boss had become generalized and it permeated her life.

She began self-hypnosis and by and by it occurred to her that she might offer her services as an independent consultant. But was she really assertive enough to do this? As she became intrigued with the possibility she found herself dropping things, forgetting things, and misplacing things. Her Inner Guide, having provided a new solution, was now creating the necessary complex stimuli that would allow changes in some of her longstanding habit patterns, changes that would enhance her ability to work independently. Inhibitions that she had not been aware of but which had caused shyness and indecisiveness abated and she became more confident and outgoing. When she had acquired enough clients, she was able to leave her salaried position and achieve fulfillment as an entrepreneur.

Working for yourself enhances comfort for several reasons.

With more opportunity to set your own timetable, you have much more control of your stimulus level. When you need a break you can take one and when you seek a higher level of stimulation you can apply yourself to your work as intensely as you wish. Also, when you have a boss, no matter how nice he might be, the reality of his authority evokes the subliminal memory pathways of past authority figures (parents, teachers, and others) who have at times been sources of discomfort. These memories, though usually subliminal, create disturbance in the present. They are typically experienced as a feeling of constraint while at work, usually so taken for granted that it is not recognized as a problem. When you are your own boss, you avoid this source of discomfort. In addition, the creativity involved in working for yourself is a source of positive stimulation. Moments of not knowing, which cause disequilibration, are followed by feelings of excitement and satisfaction as the disturbance is resolved. Creativity is health promoting, because the expansion of mental pathways contributes to an optimal level of comfort.

* * *

Nathan developed panic attacks after having been robbed at gunpoint. He had always been anxious but had never realized that it might be possible to feel otherwise. Although medication ameliorated the acute attacks, he continued to feel the anxiety that had always been with him. In psychotherapy he recalled the fear he had felt as a boy toward his father who frequently lost his temper and struck him. After finishing college, Nathan had taken a job far from his childhood home. He rarely visited and rarely thought about his family. As the memories of his father's abuse came back to him his anxiety lessened and, although he continued taking the medication, he otherwise felt ready to manage on his own.

Several years later, still on the medication, he returned to therapy complaining that his anxiety had never completely disappeared. He wondered if something more could be done for him. I told him about the new self-hypnotic technique I had developed and he responded that he had been wondering whether hypnosis might help him. He was primed for it, eager to use it, and quickly established a regular schedule. Within a couple of months his Inner Guide began communicating with him by inner thought and finger signals. Soon Nathan noticed that he was losing the passivity that had always been a part of his character. It felt very good to become more assertive and to stick up for what he needed and wanted. About a year after beginning self-hypnosis his Inner Guide told him that he no longer needed to see me. There were additional things he would learn about his childhood, things that had been split off, that would explain the anxiety and cause it to abate. His Inner Guide would make these things known to him in time. It would take quite awhile and he would continue to need the medication but he would no longer need me.

As an Inner Guide determines the sources of problems, accesses true solutions for them, and works to decrease their novelty so that they enter awareness, it takes over some of the functions of a therapist. When an individual develops sufficient trust in his Inner Guide and no longer needs his therapist to serve as a supportive and/or transference figure, he no longer needs to continue in psychotherapy. His Inner Guide can complete the work necessary to provide maximum emotional comfort.

* * *

Olivia felt shaky inside, as though she were coming apart. She looked to her friends and colleagues for support but as she described her interactions with them I could see that she was typically more perceptive and knowledgeable than they were. When I would point this out, she couldn't understand. All she knew was that she wasn't getting all that she needed from them. Because she felt threatened by the prospect of losing them, she behaved obsequiously toward them. She grew to depend on me and felt as though she would never be able to emancipate herself from therapy.

When I explained to her the new technique I had developed, she was willing to try it. She did self-hypnosis conscientiously and gradually realized that she didn't really care for these colleagues and friends. They seemed superficial to her. She was, in fact, a more caring person and much more invested in her work than they were. However, she was not comfortable on the job because of increasing demands for productivity that eroded the quality of everyone's work there. She investigated new job possibilities and found a situation that she felt would be a great improvement but it was in a different state. She felt for the first time that she could leave her family, who had not treated her well, but how could she leave me? I told her to consult with her Inner Guide who, to her shock, told that she should make the move. She didn't need me any more. She had time to absorb this knowledge as she prepared for her move and after she had relocated she wrote to tell me how happy she was with her new situation.

Olivia had a genetically determined inner instability and needed external support. Her friends had served this purpose. As she grew to depend on me and no longer needed them, she was able to view them more realistically. Now I had become the crucial support. As her Inner Guide developed, however, it was able to take over that function and she no longer needed to depend on something external to herself.

* * *

Polly felt ill at ease with people. Although she had a few friends at work whom she enjoyed, she felt estranged from most of her co-workers. They socialized and gossiped in small groups that she was not a part of and, indeed, didn't have time for. She was dedicated to her work, whereas they seemed to be more interested in getting through the day. When she did speak with them they were unresponsive and reacted as though they thought she was a little strange. At these times she felt frustrated and bewildered. She thought they were rude, yet wondered whether something was wrong with her. This uncertainty about her behavior extended to all aspects of her life. In many situations she felt at sea, unsure as to whether she was relating to people appropriately. As she described her upbringing it became clear that her mother was strange in a variety of ways. She was reclusive, moralistic, financially irresponsible, and personally unkempt.

Several months after Polly began self-hypnosis, her Inner Guide began communicating with her by inner thought and finger signals. It explained to Polly that although it was not obvious, her mother was psychotic. While her mother had interacted with her verbally, she had been unable to form an emotional bond with her. Polly, a normal child, expected and made many attempts to form a connection with her mother. When there was no response she felt depressed, angry, bewildered, and a vague discomfort that came of not understanding what was wrong.

Now, as she continued self-hypnosis, she came to appreciate that the cliques of women who were so unwelcoming found her strange because they didn't share her values or dedication. The reason that she had previously felt bewildered and wondered whether the problem lay with her was because their attitude evoked the old, locked-in response to being unresponded to, the bewilderment that had originally occurred when she was not responded to by her mother. Her Inner Guide was able to replace the old response with a new solution: Polly realized that she wouldn't enjoy the company of these women and that she didn't really want to spend time with them. She preferred the company of the friends she already had. As her Inner Guide continued her work, Polly became able to perceive situations clearly and grew confident in her capacity to relate to people appropriately.

It is important for the child of an impaired parent to understand that the parent is abnormal. Painful though this is, it eventually resolves what would otherwise be an unending disequilibration of the kind that Polly experienced.

* * *

Rob suffered from pain in his stomach. It had occurred intermittently for years but had worsened recently. He sought medical help but his doctor could find no physical cause and referred him to me. When he began self-hypnosis, the first change he noticed was that he began asserting himself with his relatives and friends. He came to realize that previously he had been unable to, and he now felt increasingly liberated. But the most acute source of distress was the stomach pain, which gradually increased.

One day during self-hypnosis, he experienced a sensation of being immobilized. His head tipped backward and his arms felt pinned to his sides. Sensing that this position had significance, he didn't attempt to move but he wondered what it meant. By and by he recalled a story that he had been told about himself. When he was a toddler he had choked on some food and turned blue, unable to breathe. His uncle, a physician who had been dining with his family that evening, performed an emergency tracheotomy. Rob now realized that he was reliving a portion of that experience.

His body gradually relaxed and as he continued in the self-hypnotic state, his thoughts wandering, he began thinking about the upcoming scuba diving trip his friends had talked him into. He had felt a strange reluctance to accompany them but didn't understand why and had agreed to go. It now occurred to him that he was afraid of going deep underwater with the scuba gear. What if he were unable to breathe? The pain in his stomach worsened. It felt as though something cold were squeezing it very tightly. He realized that the pain was caused by fear. He was terrified of being unable to breathe. It occurred to him that he didn't have to go on this trip; he was free to change his mind. The pain gradually subsided. He understood that stimuli which were related to that early event would evoke a portion of the memory: the fear, and that although his Inner Guide was surely working on this problem, it would take awhile for it to be resolved. For the time being he could take good care of himself by avoiding, where possible, stimuli that would evoke this reaction.

The pain that Rob had been feeling in his stomach, caused by fear, was a partial flashback of the early traumatic choking experience during which he had been terrified. The flashback was evoked whenever stimuli occurred that were reminiscent of the original experience. With the support of his newly acquired Inner Guide, he was able to tolerate a bit more of the experience. Thus, his head had tipped back and his arms had felt like they were pinned to his sides. These additional sensations were sufficient to stimulate the memory of the story he had been told about his choking and for him to understand the origin of his pain. His Inner Guide will repetitively think about the true solution to the trauma (namely, that it is now over) until its novelty wanes sufficiently to enter the awareness of the split off pathway that contains the memory of the original trauma.

* * *

Steve had been mildly depressed for as long as he could remember. He felt overburdened at work and although he put in very long hours he was passed over for promotion. A woman he had been attracted to for a long time hadn't been interested in him and had married someone else. He blamed himself for these problems and felt guilty for not living up to his expectations for himself. When he made mistakes he chastised himself, then engaged in compulsive cleaning rituals to try to make things right.

He was haunted by an incident that had occurred when he was four years old. He had accidentally closed the car door on his baby sister's hand and it had been permanently deformed. His mother had blamed him at the time and the ongoing sight of his sister's deformity served as a permanent reminder of his action. As he grew up he often wished that he could live that moment over again so that his sister's hand would be normal and he could feel free. As it was, he was burdened with a feeling of "heaviness" that became second nature.

Some time after beginning self-hypnosis a thought came to his mind: "It wasn't my fault." It occurred to him that he was a very little boy when the accident had happened and he now realized, looking back on it with an adult's perspective, that his mother should have been supervising more closely. His feeling of heaviness and the chronic feelings of depression gradually disappeared and he became more effective and self-confident at work.

Feelings of guilt, distressing though they are, can serve as a partial solution to a disturbance. The highly traumatic nature of the injury to Steve's sister constituted a very powerful stimulus and the daily sight of his sister's hand as he grew up served as an ongoing one. Other errors, because they were associatively related to the accident, were matched with feelings of guilt. As this response became generalized it accompanied all of Steve's thoughts and feelings, competing with and diluting them. As the novelty of his new realization waned, he felt increasingly unburdened and more able to focus clearly on his thoughts and feelings. He became more effective and much more comfortable.

* * *

Tom, an acquaintance, is a successful businessman who enjoys his work and his relationships. He has never felt the need for psychotherapy, as he has never experienced psychiatric symptoms. When he heard about the Inner Guide, however, he was intrigued and sensed that it might help him. He initially had some difficulty finding a time to do self-hypnosis because he was so busy but he finally settled on first thing in the morning, before the demands of the day crowded in.

Several weeks after beginning he saw an image of a man sitting silently and peacefully. As he continued with self-hypnosis he noticed that he felt influenced to slow down his hectic pace. Everything that needed to get done still got done. When subordinates made errors, he no longer got angry. After an initial feeling of irritation, he calmly guided them to repair whatever damage they had caused. One worker's incompetence seemed beyond remediation. Tom had been avoiding the inevitable because the prospect of firing this man made him nervous. Now, he let the man go.

At home, he had pushed his children to excel at school to increase their chances of getting into top colleges. Now, he saw that this had been counterproductive. It just made them anxious. He reflected on how wonderful they were: intelligent, creative, loving, funny. One of his sons had a learning disability and, although he had been receiving tutoring for a long time, his progress had been mediocre. Previously, Tom had been impatient for his son to "catch up." One day during self-hypnosis, as he was thinking about his son, he felt an intense sadness. He realized that his son might never be able to read and do math as competently as others. He then experienced a powerful feeling of love and compassion for him and a fierce determination to support him and help him find his own way in the world. His son might need to take an unconventional path but he could still have a rewarding life.

After providing the initial image of itself, which portrayed a characteristic that Tom needed to develop, his Inner Guide chose to work silently. Others had suggested to him that he slow down but he had not absorbed their advice. Rather than repeating these suggestions, his Inner Guide worked by allowing true solutions to surface in the form of changes in behavior and, in the case of Tom's son, by providing intense feelings that were much more powerful than words.

* * *

Vic was quick to take offense when he felt that he had been mistreated and he was always on the alert for this possibility. If someone failed to return a greeting he felt as though he had been deliberately snubbed. Whenever colleagues talked about an accomplishment that he didn't share or a possession that he didn't have, he felt that they were rubbing it in. On occasions in which he was excluded from a high-level meeting, he took it as a put down. Most distressing of all, the head of his department was patronizing, causing him to seethe with anger whenever they were together. He felt obliged to keep his feelings to himself for fear people would take further advantage if they were aware of his sensitivity.

He had been very sensitive throughout his development, although he was not aware of this himself. To him it felt normal. But as a result, he experienced every rejection, criticism, and insult especially keenly. This situation was aggravated by a number of early experiences of rejection and discrimination. As these experiences accumulated, their reverberations caused an ongoing feeling of injury and a growing state of vigilance and suspicion.

Because the difficulties seemed to come from outside himself, Vic was skeptical about the usefulness of self-hypnosis but was willing to give it a try. As his Inner Guide developed, finger signals and inner thought were established. One day, after an enraging encounter with his patronizing superior, he asked his Inner Guide what could be done about this situation. His Inner Guide replied that this man was not intentionally patronizing. He had developed this trait as a result of his own early upbringing but was unaware of it and didn't intend to put people down. Vic was amazed and felt some relief. As time passed he came to realize that many of the actions that had distressed him were not intended to be hurtful and were not to be taken personally. He was able to relax his vigilance and, as he did, he felt increasingly free and came to see the world as a place he could enjoy.

Vic's problem is common, especially for those who are very sensitive. Intense reactions to early hurts such as rejections, criticisms, teasing, and bullying lead to an ongoing disequilibration that results in a view that the world is a hurtful place.

With this expectation, any stimulus that could possibly be interpreted as malicious will be experienced so, and even neutral stimuli will come to be felt as harmful. Partial solutions to this situation include self-isolation and anger which, in order to maintain their efficacy, become more intense and elaborated over time. In some cases the need for increased intensity results in suicide or homicide. Fortunately, the majority who suffer from this problem don't reach that extremity.

* * *

These examples illustrate results that have been achieved by people I know. You can attain the results you would like by doing self-hypnosis regularly. Learning to enter the self-hypnotic state is not difficult, but persistence with it is best maintained with the help of external stimulation and support. I will offer some suggestions for how to arrange that, but first, some of you may be wondering whether your emotional distress is serious enough to warrant treatment by a mental health professional. The next chapter describes the kinds of emotional distress that would benefit from therapy.

CHAPTER 9

DO YOU NEED A THERAPIST?

I HAVE DESCRIBED how the Inner Guide can help you to take good care of yourself, manage unpleasant stimuli, and fulfill your potential for work and love. But what if you have symptoms of an emotional disorder? And what are they? Do you need a therapist?

People seek help from a mental health professional when their coping mechanisms fail in response to an unmanageable stimulus that results in distressing symptoms. The stimulus that precipitates this failure may be obvious or it may be unrecognized. For example, a person may be overwhelmed by the death of a loved one or by the subliminal perception that a loved one's health has begun to fail. Unrecognized precipitants are very common. An event, a person, an object, a place, a time of day or year, all may serve as precipitants.

Some precipitants are single events while others comprise a series of incidents. For instance, a person may be overwhelmed by the death of a loved one or after a series of failed relationships.

A stimulus that overwhelms one person may be manageable by another. For example, the loss of a loved one may trigger a clinical depression in some individuals but not in others.

Some degree of anxiety is evoked whenever we experience a change and some level of depression occurs whenever we experience a loss. These are normal responses. You will expect to feel anxious if you are promoted or to feel depressed (and anxious) if you are laid off. When a stimulus is overwhelming, however, partial and false solutions intensify until a clinical syndrome develops.

ANXIETY DISORDERS

Anxiety may escalate to panic, accompanied by physical signs such as dry mouth, rapid heartbeat, shaking, feelings of faintness or unreality, and a fear of losing control or of dying. Sometimes a person in the throes of a panic attack may feel suicidal. Once having appeared, panic attacks may recur frequently and unexpectedly. This syndrome is known as panic disorder. Fear may become attached to certain specific circumstances, such as certain locations, resulting in a need to avoid those places. This problem may generalize to a point where a person is unable to go anywhere alone, a condition called agoraphobia. Or the anxiety may attach itself to a specific object, such as a particular animal, or an experience, such as flying. A specific phobia, though intense while it is being experienced, may cause minimal disruption in a person's life if it is not encountered frequently.

Anxiety may be channeled into an obsession, that is, a repetitive series of thoughts about an unrealistic concern, such as an exaggerated fear of germs. An obsession is often accompanied by a corresponding compulsion, such as repetitive hand washing. Obsessions and compulsions can become so time-consuming that they interfere with an individual's activities and cause a great deal of distress. These anxiety disorders can be treated successfully with certain medications as well as with psychotherapy. If you are experiencing a painful degree of anxiety from any of these conditions, you can get help by seeking treatment and you can do self-hypnosis at the same time.

DEPRESSIVE DISORDERS

Feelings of sadness or depression in response to a loss may be accompanied by preoccupation with the loss and difficulty concentrating on other things. You may experience insomnia, poor appetite, and the loss of a few pounds. These symptoms usually diminish with time. They can intensify, however, to become a major depressive episode: a clinical depression.

When this occurs the insomnia becomes severe, poor appetite and weight loss continue, the degree of preoccupation results in a slowing of speech and physical movement, there is difficulty with everyday functioning, and thoughts may turn toward suicide. If you should become clinically depressed it is imperative that you get help promptly. Antidepressant medications and psychotherapy can restore your health. You won't feel motivated or have the energy to do self-hypnosis while you are clinically depressed. But you may begin or resume it as soon as you feel that you would like to, while continuing your therapy until you have recovered.

Sometimes significant depression takes another form known as dysthymia. This consists of a chronic feeling of depression accompanied by low energy and difficulty maintaining interest in one's life. Although it may include poor appetite and difficulty sleeping, it often involves the opposite: overeating and excessive sleeping. Individuals with dysthymia often don't realize that they have a disorder. They may feel that this is the way life is. They may not seek help unless another disturbance occurs. Dysthymia too can be treated with medication and psychotherapy, and self-hypnosis can be done simultaneously.

SOMATIC SYMPTOMS

Some people experience emotionally generated physical discomfort. Gastrointestinal symptoms and various kinds of pain are common expressions of such distress, and the onset of blindness, paralysis, or similar deficits may also be of emotional origin. In such cases, physical examination and laboratory tests reveal no abnormality, yet the discomfort or disability is very real. Doctors may refer these individuals to mental health professionals. Some people will be upset by such a referral because they are afraid to acknowledge that their problem might have an emotional origin. They remain convinced that they have a medical problem. If you have or if you develop such a condition you do need a therapist. Many people who have this experience are, in fact, quite relieved to learn that they are not physically ill. Here too self-hypnosis can be done in addition to psychotherapy.

Some individuals are hypochondriacal. They imagine that they are ill or exaggerate the importance of minor discomforts. They may seek medical help frequently for inconsequential symptoms. Other individuals, however, may deny the existence or significance of symptoms that should be evaluated, symptoms that are sometimes life threatening! When in doubt, visit a physician. It is better to be safe than sorry. Your Inner Guide, once it is well developed, will know when it is necessary to consult a doctor.

PERSONALITY DISORDERS

There is a condition that is not well understood and about which there are a number of explanatory theories. It is difficult even to describe this disorder because the partial and false solutions that are generated in response to its disturbance vary greatly from one person to another. Some who have experienced this condition are occasionally able to describe a feeling that surfaces when coping mechanisms are strained or fail. This feeling has been variously described as a sense of crumbling inside, of falling into an abyss, of emptiness, of being lost, or that the self is disappearing.

The most adaptive partial and false solutions include dependence on another person, maintenance of a structured environment, and denial or avoidance of the feeling of disintegration. When these solutions become unavailable, for instance when the important other leaves or the habitual structure is lost, the individual attempts to compensate by other means. They may try to regain or replace the lost person. They may feel numb or unreal, use alcohol or other drugs to blot out the reality, experience anger and depression, engage in various types of impulsive behavior to discharge tension and to serve as a distraction, or escape by means of suicidal thoughts and sometimes actions.

A frequent cause of the loss of external structure for such individuals is the expectation of autonomous functioning that begins in adolescence. For example, when Will went to college, he left behind the daily connection to his family members and the structure of his home and high school. He was on his own in the dorm, which had few regulations, and his class schedule left openings in his day. He became anxious and depressed, found himself unable to concentrate on his studies, and began experimenting with various drugs. He developed feelings of being unreal and had suicidal impulses. He required hospitalization, after which he left college, returned home, and eventually began working as a clerk in a warehouse.

Another common cause of decompensation is the loss of a partner. Yvonne has had a number of boyfriends since leaving home. In fact, she is never without one for long. Each time a man leaves her she becomes very disequilibrated. She thinks frantically and continuously about how to get him back, calling frequently and leaving notes for him. She drinks too much wine, misses days of work, and has trouble sleeping. While continuing to pursue him, she also goes to bars in hopes of meeting someone new. In short order she does and as a new relationship begins her frenzy subsides. Because of her need for a new man, any man, his personality and character are less important to her than his availability. The men in her life invariably detach themselves from her because they cannot tolerate her neediness for long.

People such as Yvonne often seek therapy, sometimes quite urgently. Some use the therapist only as a stand-in until they find a new partner. Others develop an ongoing therapeutic relationship in which, although they talk about their problems and sometimes understand their transferences, the underlying and most important therapeutic benefit is the support they receive. Some individuals, such as Will, require hospitalization, following which they may remain in therapy. Sometimes, however, if a person has had very difficult experiences with caretakers early in life, the closeness of a therapeutic relationship may feel threatening. In such cases, an important task for the therapist is to correctly understand the degree of emotional distance that the patient needs and to provide the level of connection that the patient is most comfortable with in terms of content, intensity, and spacing of appointments.

There are many different patterns of symptoms that occur in response to this disturbance. That being so, if one has symptoms, how can one know whether they are responses to this disorder? It is not always possible to tell. One sign is the need for an unusual degree of support, such as an inability to leave home. Another indication is a feeling of intense agitation during periods of loss or change. People with this condition can benefit from the structure and connection of a therapeutic relationship but, because it is usually not curative, many remain in therapy for long periods of time.

At first I wondered whether self-hypnosis would be appropriate for such people. I thought that the experience of forgoing external stimulation in order to enter the hypnotic state, and also the experience of losing awareness, might resemble the unnerving feeling of emptiness, crumbling, or loss of a sense of self. I then realized that some people with this condition had already done meditation without ill effect so I offered self-hypnosis to those of my patients with this disorder. I expected only that an Inner Guide might help them to better manage their situation and their symptoms but, in fact, they were able to achieve autonomy. I hypothesize that the Inner Guide, a strong internal presence, is able to replace the previously needed external supports or even that it fills in an internal deficiency, providing a crucial element that completes the mental structure. Individuals with this disorder should be in therapy until they can achieve autonomy through self-hypnosis.

PSYCHOSES

The psychoses are severe mental disorders in which individuals lose touch with reality and become unable to function. Schizophrenia is manifested predominantly by cognitive symptoms that may be primarily "positive," such as delusions and hallucinations, or "negative," such as marked diminution of feeling and action. With treatment there are usually, but not always, periods of remission, some quite lengthy, and there are reports of cures in treatment.

A bipolar disorder is manifested principally by periods of altered mood. During manic episodes a person experiences elevation of mood, typically with a speeding up of ideas, speech, and actions that, coupled with the loss of judgment, can have very deleterious results. The individual may overspend or develop grandiose plans that, if executed, result in loss of assets, or may engage in sexual indiscretions. A bipolar disorder may consist entirely of manic episodes or it may comprise an array of manic, depressive, and mixed episodes. Usually there are periods of normal mood and functioning, often lengthy, between the episodes of decompensation.

Because psychotic symptoms may at times result from physical illness or substance misuse, it is important that individuals manifesting these symptoms receive a medical evaluation. People with psychotic disorders sometimes realize that they need help, but more often it is their relatives and friends who bring them for treatment. There are medications that can be very effective in ameliorating the symptoms of these conditions, and psychotherapy is important, as well. Individuals with these disorders should be in therapy. If such individuals wish to do self-hypnosis during periods of remission, they will benefit.

DISSOCIATIVE DISORDERS

Those who experience problematic signs of dissociation, such as frequent traumatic nightmares, recurring episodes of sleepwalking, periods of amnesia, fugue states, prolonged depersonalization, or frequent flashbacks, should seek treatment. So too should those with stress disorders, in which a traumatic event is followed by a variety of distressing symptoms that include repetitive re-experiencing (in dreams or flashbacks), avoidance of associated stimuli (limiting thoughts, feelings, and actions), and significant anxiety (including insomnia, hypervigilance, and a tendency to startle easily). People with these conditions should be in therapy but they also can use self-hypnosis to develop an Inner Guide.

There is one condition for which preliminary therapeutic steps are necessary before an Inner Guide can be developed. Individuals with dissociative identity disorder have developed multiple personalities, each of which appears in response to stimuli that are specifically evocative. A stimulus that represents a threat may evoke an aggressive, protective alter, whereas a stimulus that represents abandonment may elicit a depressed, hopeless personality. A person with this condition will be leery of seeking an Inner Guide through self-hypnosis, and understandably so. If it were to be attempted, one of the personalities that has already developed would emerge. It would be whichever one had been most activated by the current internal and external stimuli.

Among the variety of alters that develop, there is one that functions as a manager of the others. It attempts to juggle their needs for expression and time "out" (that is, time during which an alter is in awareness and in control of the person's actions). This alter has been called an "Internal Self-Helper." It never comes "out" itself because its job can be fulfilled internally. In the treatment of such a patient, however, the therapist can call upon the Internal Self-Helper for aid in understanding the other alters. Responding to the stimulus of the therapist's request, the Internal Self-Helper can emerge and provide useful information.

In the treatment of patients with dissociative identity disorder the different alters emerge at different times, some more often than others, but all according to the degree to which they are stimulated. If the therapist regularly elicits the Internal Self-Helper and converses with it, it will grow and strengthen as it develops associations to many external stimuli and experiences the feeling of being real.

There will be times when the other alters come "out" as they receive strong stimuli but as the therapist focuses on developing the Internal Self-Helper, it will develop a mind of its own and a wish to become more effective at maintaining internal order. If the therapist suggests that the Internal Self-Helper attend at all times to what is happening, its co-awareness with whatever other alter is "out" at each moment will lead to their integrations: a series of true solutions. These changes, as with all others, are disequilibrating. They must be repeated until the novelty wanes and they are able to enter awareness. The integrated personality will then be able to develop its Inner Guide as others do.

People with dissociative identity disorder are, before treatment, usually unaware that they have this condition. If they seek therapy, it is most often for depression, anxiety, or physical symptoms. If they are brought for treatment by others, it may be for dissociative symptoms, substance misuse, or suicidal tendencies. It is important for the therapist to consider the possibility of this condition when treatments for presenting symptoms are not successful or if certain telltale phenomena have been experienced, such as dreamlike memories or gaps in the memory, lost time, out-of-body experiences, internal conversation or argument, or flashbacks. These patients may also experience puzzling occurrences such as finding themselves with possessions they didn't buy or finding evidence of actions that they were not aware of performing. Although the treatment for this disorder is psychotherapy, one or more of the alters may themselves have conditions, such as anxiety or depression, that can be treated with medication.

Sometimes patients with dissociative identity disorder and others who have been abused want to confront their past abusers or even sue or bring criminal charges against them to express their anger, get justice or revenge, or gain a sense of mastery. While action may be desirable to protect new victims if the past abuser is still active, it is otherwise better to refrain because the resulting intense restimulation will prolong the reverberation of the trauma and delay the achievement of emotional comfort.

* * *

People with conditions described in this chapter may benefit from both medication and psychotherapy. Although the mechanisms of medications for emotional disorders are not yet fully understood, it has been clearly demonstrated that they are often effective. The physiological changes that they cause in the brain result in alterations in an individual's thoughts and feelings, and amelioration of mental distress. Conversely, it has been shown that mental activity, thoughts and feelings, can cause changes in the anatomy and physiology of the brain. Mind-brain relationships are incompletely understood at this time but we are fortunate to have both pharmacological and psychological treatments for the emotional disorders that have been described in this chapter.

If you have one of these disorders, you should seek treatment. If you aren't sure whether or not you do, you can arrange for an evaluation by a mental health professional. Therapy will provide relief and it will also serve as a support as you begin doing self-hypnosis.

Most people who want to develop an Inner Guide will need periodic encouragement at first in order to continue with self-hypnosis until they begin to experience the changes that will make them more comfortable. The next chapter describes some of the ways that you can arrange this kind of support for yourself.

CHAPTER 10

AN INVITATION!

AS I HAVE described, there are five stages in the process of developing one's Inner Guide.

The first stage involves becoming comfortable with and confident in one's ability to enter the self-hypnotic state. For most people this is soon accomplished, often during the first session.

The second stage consists of establishing the habit of doing self-hypnosis. This is most reliably accomplished by devising a regular schedule for it. Often one's first idea of the best schedule doesn't work out and alternative times must be tried. Even those of my patients who are very busy or who are surrounded by other people most of the time have found workable situations for doing self-hypnosis.

The third stage consists of the period of time from settling into a workable schedule until communication with the Inner Guide is achieved. This period of time is quite variable. Some make contact within a few weeks or months. For others, the prospect of communication is so overstimulating that it may not occur until they are far along in the process.

125

For my patients, the fourth stage includes the period of time from the onset of communication until the individual develops sufficient trust and confidence in the Inner Guide so that I am no longer needed. For those who will not achieve communication early on, it would be from the time a workable schedule is established. At this point, the Inner Guide has become more helpful than I can be. It knows more about the patient's life and situation than I do and can provide the best possible solutions for problems. It is at this point that my patients end treatment.

For you, the end-point of the fourth stage will come when you can confidently depend on your Inner Guide to provide the best solutions for your problems.

As I have mentioned, for some people the end points of the third and fourth stages may come in reverse order. I have had patients who have improved to the point where they have felt ready to leave even before direct communication with the Inner Guide has occurred. I know that they will ultimately achieve this connection because it is part of the Inner Guide's means of providing maximum emotional comfort.

The fifth stage covers the remaining time until all maladaptive habit patterns have abated. When this point is reached, the individual's baseline stimulus level is optimal and new disequilibrations are handled with maximum efficiency.

REINFORCEMENT

Although the complete process occurs over a period of several years, you will begin to notice changes for the better after the first few months. Because the results do take some time to appear, however, the most difficult aspect of this technique will be persisting in the absence of immediate reward. This difficulty is understandable. We know from learning theory that unrewarded behaviors are extinguished; they diminish and cease. For my patients, friends, and relatives, continuing contact with me has provided them with the necessary stimulation to continue. But how can you provide yourself with similar reinforcement? You will need it.

Talking with others about self-hypnosis will help. Talking is a stronger, more reinforcing stimulus than thinking, because an act provides stimuli of sensation in addition to those of thought and feeling.

If your Inner Guide has chosen to communicate with you, talking with it will provide reinforcement for both of you. The more your Inner Guide communicates with you, the more real it will feel. That will increase the efficacy of its work, as well as providing you with additional stimulation.

Another way to provide reinforcement is to link self-hypnosis with another activity. For example, some writers use meditation for inspiration. They find that meditation produces images that make excellent beginnings for stories. A writer could enter self-hypnosis in the usual way, following the technique I have described, in order to evoke his Inner Guide. Once that has occurred, he would then be free to wait for an image to write about while his Inner Guide continues its work. Perhaps you can find a way to link self-hypnosis with one or more of your activities.

Another possibility might be to create a group that meets regularly. Others who would like to use this technique could share experiences and help each other with any difficulties that they experience. Or you could incorporate these objectives into a group already formed for some other purpose, such as a book club or weight-loss program.

You may find, as some have, that developing a schedule or routine for doing self-hypnosis can become a stumbling block. What might prevent you from establishing this habit? You may start out with good intentions but then begin to taper off. I have come to realize that people who do this experience self-hypnosis as a chore rather than an adventure. They have not yet felt rewarding changes or communicated with their Inner Guide. The feeling of relaxation loses its novelty and so too does the anticipation of solutions to discomforts. When one doesn't yet know what the solutions will be there is nothing to hold the attention. One cannot think for long about an unknown. A vision is needed.

It will be helpful to think about the Inner Guide itself because it is something that can be visualized. Although the initial image may be inaccurate, it is concrete. In most instances the true image will be a representation of your ideal self. What would you like for that to be? What will it look like? What will it sound like? What might it say to you? What might you say to it? You can begin talking to your Inner Guide silently, so as not to bring yourself out of self-hypnosis, even before it makes contact with you. Your vision of it can help to tide you over the first weeks or months of self-hypnosis until you begin experiencing its effects.

You could also receive periodic stimulation and encouragement from me by subscribing to the biweekly Letter that is published by The Davis Foundation for Providing Emotional Comfort. The Letters contain additional information about the theory and technique, examples of the Inner Guide's activity, answers to questions received from those who are doing self-hypnosis, and occasional book reviews. You are invited to subscribe to the Letter by contacting The Davis Foundation for Providing Emotional Comfort. You may wish to visit its web site, as well.

> The Davis Foundation for Providing
> Emotional Comfort
> Suite 1125
> 30 North Michigan Avenue
> Chicago, Illinois 60602
> (312) 230-0114
> www.davis-foundation.org

In addition, please feel free to contact me directly at my web site, jd@judithdavis.com.

I wish you the very best. I know that when you develop your Inner Guide, you will achieve a degree of emotional comfort that you would never have imagined. You will develop a level of creativity that will bring you tremendous satisfaction.

AFTERWORD

As YOU ACHIEVE maximum emotional comfort, you will develop the skills and resources that will enable you to provide for yourself and your loved ones while doing something that you find very meaningful and enjoyable. This may, but not necessarily, involve a change of occupation. You will also enhance your capacity for gaining great pleasure from the interests of your leisure time. What next?

Having found true solutions for your own problems, you will find yourself becoming interested in solving the problems of others and of the world in general. Why? Because even total peace becomes uncomfortable after awhile. Your mind will continue to require new challenges in order to maintain the optimal level of stimulation. If this concept seems burdensome, it is merely an indication that you presently feel weighed down by problems that are not yet solved. When the time comes, you will look forward to new challenges.

Through the ages, our civilization has made amazing advances in many areas but human nature has not changed. Now we have the means to transform personality as well. As people use this self-hypnotic technique, their increasing comfort will cause traits such as greed, envy, and hostility to subside, while qualities such as sensitivity to others, generosity, and creativity grow. In time, we can make the world a much more comfortable place.

FREQUENTLY ASKED QUESTIONS

WHAT IS SELF-HYPNOSIS?

Q. How is self-hypnosis different from meditation?
A. There are two differences. First is the method. When people meditate, they often use guided imagery or repeat a word or phrase over and over. In self-hypnosis, we focus on an unchanging spot in order to minimize stimuli until the Inner Guide is activated. Then we are free to think about whatever we want.

The second difference has to do with what one wishes to develop. People who meditate may be seeking any number of results, whereas in self-hypnosis we seek a very specific entity: the Inner Guide.

Q. Will it help to use imagery or repeat a phrase like people do with meditation?
A. No. While entering the self-hypnotic state, imagery and phrases are stimuli that will interfere with the goal of diminishing all stimuli as much as possible. Once in the state, it doesn't matter what one thinks about. The Inner Guide is at work in its pathway.

Who Can Do Self-Hypnosis?

Q. Can anybody do self-hypnosis and benefit from it?
A. Anyone who wants to develop an Inner Guide and who doesn't feel threatened by the idea can do so and benefit. People

who have great difficulty concentrating on one thing for a short period of time may need extra help in the beginning.

Certain people have developed a habit pattern of maintaining control of themselves and those around them. They may not necessarily be aware that they do this. They may not care for self-hypnosis because it involves relinquishing control.

People with significant symptoms of emotional distress, as described in chapter 10, should do self-hypnosis only in the context of, and with the support of, a therapeutic situation.

Q. Can I suggest self-hypnosis to my relatives and friends?
A. You can tell them about it. If they find it interesting, they may want to do it themselves. However, if the idea seems to make them apprehensive, don't pursue it with them. They aren't ready for it.

Q. At what age can a child begin self-hypnosis to develop an Inner Guide?
A. When the child expresses an interest in doing so and is able to understand the concept of the Inner Guide. The child needs to be able to understand the abstract concept that when the mind registers a perception, it breaks that perception up into its component parts and stores these parts in different mental pathways. The child needs to comprehend that one such pathway is composed of all the experiences of comfort, and that the Inner Guide will be composed of this pathway, a sense of its own identity, and the wish to provide maximum emotional comfort.

A child should never be pressured into trying self-hypnosis. Not only will the child be made uncomfortable but, under pressure, self-hypnosis won't work.

WHAT IS THE INNER GUIDE?

Q. I already meditate and I have an inner voice that helps me. It answers questions and gives advice. Isn't that my Inner Guide?
A. No. Many people who meditate have developed various kinds of inner voices, advisors, or spirits. When people meditate, they will get whatever they wish for. The Inner Guide is a very specific entity. It is a combination of three things: (1) the mental pathway consisting of all the memories of past experiences of comfort, (2) the wish to help you, and (3) a sense of its own identity.

Q. Isn't one just creating an Inner Guide through suggestion?
A. Yes, indeed! The primordial Inner Guide is the mental pathway consisting of the memories of comfort. If you wish for it to grow and become helpful, it will.

Q. Can I develop my Inner Guide by wishing for it without bothering to do self-hypnosis?
A. No. Self-hypnosis provides the necessary conditions under which it can develop.

Q. Is the Inner Guide like a spirit from outside that is contacting me, like a deceased person, or something religious or mystical?
A. No, the Inner Guide doesn't come from the outside. It's a part of your own mind.

Q. The concept of the Inner Guide seems weird, spooky, strange.
A. Yes, it may seem quite foreign at first. It certainly did to me. It's so different from anything in our previous experience.

Q. If the Inner Guide is wiser than I am, why doesn't it just take over and live my life for me?
A. The Inner Guide doesn't have that capability. It is only a part of you. It needs you just as much as you need it.

ENTERING THE SELF-HYPNOTIC STATE

Q. I don't think I'm really doing self-hypnosis because when I try to do it, I feel the same as I usually do.
A. You will feel almost the same. The only difference is that you will feel more relaxed than usual. You may not notice that until you come out of the state and find yourself very relaxed.

Q. I don't think I'm really doing self-hypnosis because I just keep thinking the same kinds of thoughts that I usually do.
A. That is normal. Once you enter the state (as your eyes close), you will resume having your usual thoughts and feelings. Simultaneously, the Inner Guide is experiencing its thoughts and feelings.

Q. How can I keep my mind clear of thoughts while in self-hypnosis?
A. You don't need to. In order to enter self-hypnosis, you focus on a spot until your eyes spontaneously close. As soon as they do, you have entered the self-hypnotic state and are free to think about anything that you would like to. Simultaneously, out of your awareness, your Inner Guide is thinking its thoughts.

Q. I don't think I'm really doing self-hypnosis because my eyes don't close.
A. Some people enter the self-hypnotic state without closing their eyes. You need only to focus on the spot. When you see an afterimage or when you feel relaxed you will have entered the self-hypnotic state. Then you can close your eyes yourself.

Q. I just stay in self-hypnosis for a few minutes. Is that enough?
A. Every moment that you are in self-hypnosis is helpful. As you continue with it you will find that you stay in longer, although the length will vary from day to day depending on

the number and strength of the other stimuli you are experiencing on that day.

GOING DEEP

Q. Why do people go deep?
A. If, during a self-hypnotic session, one's thoughts and feelings lose their novelty sufficiently, they will be unable to maintain awareness. This is how we fall asleep at night.

Q. How is going deep different from falling asleep?
A. Although we have lost awareness, the Inner Guide hasn't. It continues to think and feel. Also, our body is not physiologically asleep. That is why coming out of a deep self-hypnosis feels more sudden than waking from sleep.

Q. When I first learned self-hypnosis, I went deeper than I have since. Why is that? Does it mean that I'm not doing it right or that it won't work for me?
A. You may have gone deeper if you were taught self-hypnosis by another person because the influence of their presence may have served to intensify the experience. If you have been going less deep since, it doesn't matter. Self-hypnosis will still be effective.

Q. If I don't go deep at all, will self-hypnosis be less effective?
A. It will be just as effective. The Inner Guide has been evoked and is active in its own pathway whether or not you lose awareness in your pathway.

Q. Why do I go deep on some days but not on others?
A. It depends on the number and strength of the other stimuli that you are experiencing on that day. The more there are, the longer you will be kept in awareness as you think about them.

Q. Some days I don't go deep even though I don't feel a lot of other stimulation. Why is that?

A. There are many stimuli that you won't be aware of; some because they are subliminal and some because they are so intense that the mental apparatus keeps them out of awareness.

ESTABLISHING A ROUTINE

Q. I don't seem to be able to discipline myself to do self-hypnosis regularly. How can I get myself to do it?
A. Choose a time of day and a place that seem optimal and think of self-hypnosis as part of your daily routine. Some find it best to do it in the morning, others prefer the evening. Establishing a time and place is a matter of trial and error. Typically, a person may have to try more than one situation before finding the best one. If your first choice, the most obvious choice, doesn't work, don't be discouraged. You can find another way.

Q. I don't seem to have time to do self-hypnosis.
A. Remember that while you are doing self-hypnosis, you are free to think about whatever you wish. For example, you may want to think about a project you are developing at work, what to choose as a birthday present for a relative, or what to have for dinner. You can do mental work and accomplish things while in self-hypnosis.

Q. I was doing self-hypnosis every day but then I got so busy I stopped. How can a person keep to their schedule?
A. There may well be times when you are too busy. That's understandable. Simply resume as soon as there is time.

ESTABLISHING COMMUNICATION WITH THE INNER GUIDE

Q. If my Inner Guide is just a mental pathway, it can't communicate with me like a person, can it?

A. Yes. As it develops, it will achieve a sense of identity. It's like having a friend inside you.

Q. What will my Inner Guide look like?
A. Some Inner Guides choose not to provide an image of themselves. Others will. Occasionally, an Inner Guide may initially provide a temporary image to make a certain point. However, the image most often provided, the true image of your Inner Guide, will be a representation of your ideal self.

Q. I keep trying to get into contact with my Inner Guide but nothing happens. Am I doing something wrong?
A. No. Your Inner Guide will choose the best time to begin communicating with you.

Q. How soon after beginning self-hypnosis will I make contact with my Inner Guide?
A. The timing of contact varies greatly from one person to another. Your Inner Guide may determine that remaining silent will help maintain the optimal level of disequilibration. Or it may be that the whole idea of contact is so overstimulating that it can't yet come into your awareness. Sometimes the Inner Guide remains silent in order to make a certain point. Some people's Inner Guides remain silent for a long time. Be assured that if your Inner Guide chooses to remain silent, it has determined that this is the most efficient way for it to help you. Contact will occur eventually.

Q. My Inner Guide is talking with me in my mind but I haven't learned to do finger signals or automatic handwriting. Do I need to do those, too?
A. Yes, it's a good idea to develop those methods of communication. There will be times when they will be helpful.

Q. I seem to have made contact with my Inner Guide, but what should I say to it?
A. You can ask it anything you want to. Because the Inner Guide has access to subliminal perceptions, it has knowledge

of the character and intentions of the people you encounter so it can help you assess people accurately. It can also tell you things you don't know about your own character. Because it has access to your entire memory bank, it can answer many questions about the world around you and about your own past. It can provide the best available judgment concerning decisions that you make and the best possible solutions for problems. Often, your Inner Guide will choose not to answer, but when it does, you will be surprised at the new information you learn.

Q. My Inner Guide often doesn't answer my questions. Why is that?
A. The Inner Guide helps you maintain an optimal level of disequilibration. Not answering questions is one way of maintaining that level.

Q. My Inner Guide rarely talks to me. Why is that?
A. This is another way of maintaining an optimal level of disequilibration.

Q. My Inner Guide gives contradictory answers. When I ask a question, first it says "yes" and then it says "no." It doesn't seem to know what it's doing. How can I depend on it?
A. This is yet another way that the Inner Guide has of maintaining an optimal level of disequilibration. Try to put up with it. It is all in the service of helping you solve your problems.

Q. My Inner Guide can't learn how to write. It just keeps scribbling. What's wrong with it?
A. This is still another way of maintaining the optimal level of disequilibration.

Q. When my Inner Guide says things to me I'm not always sure whether it's the Inner Guide or just my own thought, especially when the answer is something that I want to hear. How do I know it isn't just my own thought?

A. Sometimes the inner thought is very obviously the Inner Guide's because it is something that you would never have thought of yourself. It will surprise you. However, there are times when you may be unsure. At times, when your Inner Guide knows that you are uncertain, it may think its thought very forcefully. If it doesn't, you can ask for confirmation with finger signals. They are more definitive because they involve a sensation: the feeling of having your finger move independently.

Q. Does it help for me to talk with my Inner Guide?
A. Yes. It helps your Inner Guide develop its sense of identity and its feeling of its own reality. If it prefers not to do this, it is because it has determined that it's more efficient to work silently.

Q. I had established contact with my Inner Guide, but now it seems to have disappeared. Is it gone for good?
A. No. It has determined that it's more efficient to work silently for a while.

ESTABLISHING TRUST

Q. How can I trust my Inner Guide?
A. It's natural that you would not immediately trust your Inner Guide because it is new to you and seems strange. Test it. Ask questions that you know the answers to and see whether it agrees. If it doesn't agree, ask it why. Ask advice on small matters in order to see whether the advice is helpful. You need to give your Inner Guide chances to prove itself to you.

Q. What if my Inner Guide is something bad that will be destructive?
A. The Inner Guide is a very positive, good entity. Remember, it is composed only of the mental pathway containing all your past experiences of comfort, a sense of its own identity, and the wish to help you.

Q. When I do self-hypnosis, I sometimes feel anx-

ious, or angry, or sad. It's uncomfortable. Is something wrong?

A. No. Many people don't have this experience but if you do just try to tolerate the feelings in order to achieve the ultimate goal. These feelings represent an integration of formerly split-off feelings with mental pathways that reach awareness. Though temporarily uncomfortable, this is part of a healing process and represents progress.

Q. If the Inner Guide will influence me to do what is best for me, will it force me to give up certain indulgences that I enjoy and don't want to give up?

A. No. The Inner Guide is not coercive. It won't force anything on you.

Q. I want to be in charge of myself. Will the Inner Guide rob me of my autonomy?

A. No. The Inner Guide wouldn't want you to lose your autonomy. Its intention is to be helpful to you. It can be so only with your cooperation.

Q. What if I don't like the Inner Guide's answers or advice?

A. You don't have to do anything you don't want to.

Along the Way

Q. How long will it take before all my problems are solved?

A. The time varies greatly from person to person. It will take several years but you will experience progress and feel increasingly better along the way.

Q. What can I do to speed up the process?

A. Your Inner Guide is working as efficiently as it can. All you can do to help is to do self-hypnosis regularly. The more often you do it, the sooner you will get results.

Q. Why is it that some of my problems have been

solved but not the one I care about the most?
A. Your Inner Guide deals with your problems in the order of their importance. Most people have problems that they are unaware of and that are more disequilibrating than the ones they know about. Also, the solutions that you want may depend on the resolution of problems you are not aware of. In due course all problems will be solved.

Q. What is speedreading and why is it useful for my Inner Guide to have information if I can't access it?
A. Speedreading means glancing at each page for a moment so that its content is registered in your memory. Unless the content is very striking, it won't make sufficient impact to enter your awareness. But because the Inner Guide has access to the entire memory bank, it can draw upon the content as needed to solve problems. For instance, if you were to skim the *Diet for Dancers* book, your Inner Guide would gain a better understanding of nutrition and would guide you to modify your eating habits in such a way that, over time, you would eat in the healthiest way possible while still enjoying your meals just as much, if not more.

* * *

Because you have wished for an Inner Guide, you have already brought it into existence. It has already determined the sources of all of your problems and discomforts and it has accessed solutions for them. All that is needed now is for you to spend enough time in self-hypnosis for these solutions to enter your awareness. I am sometimes asked, "What can I do to make this happen for me?" or told, "I'm going to work really hard at this to make it happen." I remind them that all they need to do and all that they can do, is to do self-hypnosis regularly. Their Inner Guide does the rest.

Some of my patients, relatives, friends, and people in the Davis Foundation project have been shown an image of their Inner Guide. It is usually something that they didn't expect and wouldn't have thought of themselves. It has appeared to them as a representation of their ideal self, as a powerful protector, or an intense source of love. An Inner Guide is all of that. Whether or not your Inner Guide chooses to show you an image, you should know that it loves you very much, wants to protect you and help you and, given the chance, will solve your problems and discomforts. It is your best friend.

APPENDIX:
THEORIES OF THE MIND

The theory described in this book is derived from the classical conditioning theory developed by Pavlov, and provides a new way of understanding the mind. How does it compare with psychoanalytic theories?

FREUD

Psychoanalytic theory began with Sigmund Freud, who created several models of the mind over time. The *topographical model* consists of *consciousness* (that which is in awareness at a given moment), a *preconscious* (everything in the mind that could enter awareness easily when relevant), and an *unconscious* (content that would be too upsetting to enter awareness). The unconscious is separated from the preconscious by a repression barrier (imagine a horizontal line) that works actively to keep disturbing material from surfacing and becoming conscious. The unconscious material (for example, an unacceptable sexual urge) presses for discharge, so the repression barrier must be active in holding this material back.

The new theory proposes that the mind, rather than containing a *repression barrier* that bars upsetting stimuli from reaching consciousness, has a matching function that matches such disturbances with solutions. A true solution will end the disturbance, a partial solution will diminish it, and a false solution will provide an alternative experience.

Freud saw that the young child experiences sexual urges toward the parents, a situation that he termed the *Oedipus com-*

143

plex after the ancient Greek king who, abandoned at birth and raised by others, unknowingly killed his father and married his mother. The child learns that these sexual wishes are forbidden and they become *repressed*, that is, held in the unconscious by the repression barrier. If the child is able to acknowledge the impossibility of such wishes and relinquish them, the Oedipus complex is said to be resolved.

Sometimes this does not happen and the unconscious sexual wishes for the parent remain, in which case the individual is said to be neurotic. The sexual wishes for the parent can cross the repression barrier into consciousness if they are sufficiently disguised. For example, a woman may fall in love with men who resemble her father in some way, either in terms of appearance, personality characteristics, or even in terms of unavailability (for instance, married men). These love objects are called *derivatives* because they are derived from the original love object. The woman repeats this unrewarding behavior because she is driven to do so by her unconscious sexual wishes.

The new theory views the disguises, or derivatives, as partial solutions because they allow for partial satisfaction of the sexual wishes. The woman isn't fully satisfied, however, because the wishes really have to do with her father.

Children also learn that certain aggressive wishes are forbidden, and Freud felt that these, too, are repressed. For instance, a boy who hates his father for exclusively possessing his mother will need to repress that feeling and may project the feeling onto his father so that he feels that his father hates him. Or he may fear retribution for his incestuous wishes. If this neurotic situation is not resolved, the child, upon reaching adulthood, may displace these feelings onto a male authority figure, for instance his boss, and feel intimidated by him or have unconscious wishes to kill him. The child also has loving feelings toward the parent of the same sex and hateful feelings toward the rival for that relationship. This is called the *negative Oedipus complex*.

Again, the new theory views these disguises as partial solutions for the disturbances caused by the man's forbidden feelings. According to Freud, dreams serve as wish fulfillments. Experiences from the previous day that are related to unconscious wishes are called *day residues* (for example, seeing a person who looks like a parent). They provide the disguises for the unconscious wishes that are pressing for discharge. The wishes are then able, distorted in one way or another, to cross the repression barrier and enter consciousness in the form of dreams. The distortions are caused by a variety of mechanisms, such as projection of feelings onto another ("I don't hate him, he hates me") and displacement ("I don't have romantic feelings for A, but for B").

Freud first illustrated his view of the process of dream formation by describing a dream of his own. The day preceding the dream he had experienced a veiled criticism by a colleague, Otto, of Freud's incomplete treatment of a patient he called Irma. That evening in an attempt to justify his treatment of Irma he wrote up her case history. An abbreviated version of the dream is as follows: Irma appears. Freud tells her that her incomplete cure is her own fault because she hasn't accepted his psychoanalytic interpretation. He then notices that she looks quite ill. She has recently been given an injection by Otto, which has probably caused her present condition. Otto probably used a dirty syringe.

Freud used *free association*, that is, the technique of allowing the mind to wander freely and thoughts to emerge without censorship to elucidate links between the features of the dream and the unconscious wishes. The thoughts that came to his mind revealed that he wished to absolve himself of blame for Irma's unresolved symptoms and did so by displacing the blame onto her for refusing his interpretation and onto Otto for giving her a faulty injection. Additionally, he felt that the dream satisfied a wish to attack Otto by portraying him as having caused her illness.

Freud felt that all dreams represented wish fulfillments except for the dreams that follow a traumatic experience.

These dreams, which are not disguised, replay the event, like a flashback, and occur repeatedly. He felt that they were an attempt to master the trauma retrospectively.

According to the new theory, all dreams are flashbacks. They occur in response to complex stimuli that have not been satisfactorily solved during the day and which therefore continue to be disturbing. During the day partial solutions can be chosen but during sleep these solutions are unavailable due to the absence of mobility and waking thought. False solutions are chosen and the complex stimulus oscillates with them, causing flashbacks. When Otto criticized Freud's treatment of Irma he became a complex stimulus: simultaneously friend and foe. Freud's partial solution that evening was to write a justification of his treatment of Irma. If this description were acceptable to Otto, he would no longer be able to criticize and would then no longer function as a complex stimulus. The write-up was not a true solution, because Freud's treatment of Irma was, indeed, incomplete. In the dream a false solution is chosen. By displacing the blame for Irma's incomplete cure first onto her, then Otto, Freud eliminates himself as an object of criticism. When Otto can no longer criticize him, he will revert to a simple stimulus: friend.

Another example, from my own experience: I had been frequently visiting an elderly relative in an assisted living facility who was dying. Her thinking was impaired due to a series of mini-strokes and she was failing physically. One evening she appeared inexplicably better. That night I dreamed that I was in bed with her. A nurse knocked on the door. I struggled with one hand to turn the doorknob to let the nurse in, to no avail. I then grasped the doorknob with both hands and was able to turn it. The relative's condition served as a complex stimulus: she was deteriorating yet she was better. In the dream, her condition was displaced onto me and the nature of the damage from her strokes was changed from cognitive to physical. I was trying to open the door with one hand because the other was paralyzed by stroke. By negating the stroke, I was able to use the other hand as well and succeed in opening the door. The false solutions of changing the nature of the stroke, displacing it onto myself, and negating my dysfunction succeeded in resolving the complex stimulus. There was no longer deterioration, but recovery.

Because the topographical model did not explain all the phenomena that Freud observed in his patients, he later devised the *structural model* of the mind, which consists of the *id*, the *ego* and the *superego*. The ego and the superego are partly conscious and partly located in the unconscious; the id is entirely in the unconscious. The id contains the basic drives (sex and aggression), the superego serves as the conscience, and the ego is the part of the mind that negotiates when the drives, the demands of the external environment, and the superego are in conflict.

The ego may simply cause repression, a state in which the conflict does not enter consciousness, or it may devise a *neurotic* compromise in which the drive and the defense are both represented in disguised form. This results in a symptom. For example, an unacceptable sexual drive may be handled by the creation of a *conversion symptom* that involves a change in perception. The individual may develop "hysterical blindness" (inability to see a forbidden object) or anesthesia of a limb (inability to feel a forbidden sexual feeling). An unacceptable aggressive drive may be managed by the creation of a compulsion, for example, repetitive hand washing, an attempt to get rid of a "dirty" feeling.

The new theory proposes that perceptions that are too disturbing to enter awareness are matched with either partial or false solutions. A false solution may consist simply of negating an internal perception, such as an unacceptable sexual or aggressive feeling, thus preventing it from entering awareness (Freud's "repression"). Or, the negation may be accompanied by an alternative thought, feeling, or action. Hysterical blindness, anesthesias, and compulsions are all false solutions.

In therapy, the treatment is structured to allow the development of *transference* toward the therapist; that is, to allow the therapist to become a figure upon whom the Oedipal feelings can be expressed (like the neurotic woman's unavailable man or the neurotic man's "dangerous" boss). When the patient has developed a *transference neurosis* to the therapist, it is interpreted. "You desire me as you desired your father; but I am not available, as he wasn't." Or, "You expect me to hurt you because you are experiencing me as you did your father, whom you expected would punish you for your forbidden sexual wishes toward your mother." With repeated interpretations called *working through*, the patient's neurosis is resolved and the patient can then go forward unencumbered by the past.

The new theory conceptualizes a transference figure as a stimulus that is related to the original stimulus. It evokes the same feelings as does the original stimulus but because these feelings are less disturbing in relation to the transference object, they may enter awareness. It feels less unsafe to fantasize sexual feelings toward another adult than toward the original, parental figure and it feels less dangerous to anticipate being hurt by a boss than by a parent. A transference figure is a complex stimulus, however, because it is perceived simultaneously as a transference object and a real object. Therefore, matching to it will be momentarily suspended, allowing the matching of a new solution when it is provided by the therapist. The therapist's interpretation that the patient has been reliving the past in the present, but that this is no longer necessary, provides a true solution to replace the false one. Because the implications of this solution are so momentous, it is initially very overstimulating. Repetitions of the interpretation (working through) are necessary in order that its novelty wane sufficiently so that it can enter awareness.

KLEIN

Melanie Klein, a student of Freud's, worked with children as well as adults. She developed theory about the earliest phases of life, the *preoedipal* period. While Freud focused primarily on the individual's internal urges (sexual and aggressive) and the mechanisms for handling those urges, Klein sought to understand the individual's relationships with external objects, specifically the mother. She described infants as *introjecting* (taking in) the maternal attitudes, both positive and negative, and identifying with them. Thus the good and bad aspects become part of the infant's personality. The infant initially maintains a separation between the good and the bad but eventually integrates them.

If in unfortunate cases the maternal feeling toward the infant is more negative than positive, the infant cannot integrate the two aspects for fear of being left only with the bad aspect (the stronger bad destroying the good). The *split* remains. To rid himself of the internal "badness" the individual may *project* the negative aspect onto another. He will then fear that other, who now seems dangerous. The "goodness" may be projected onto another in an attempt to acquire an external figure that is loving and protective. In treatment, the projections onto the therapist are interpreted in the same way that transferences are.

The new theory explains these phenomena in terms of the mental pathways that are formed by the positive and negative stimuli that a child experiences. Positive stimuli, such as expressions of parental love and caring, evoke feelings of pleasure, and pathways consisting of loving stimuli and pleasurable responses develop. Negative stimuli, such as parental anger, hatred, or disapproval, evoke feelings of fear, anger, and despair, and pathways of these feelings also develop.

If a parent is irritated, this stimulus may be matched with a partial solution, such as remembering that previous irritations were short-lived. If a parent is enraged, however, a terrified child may match this with a false solution, giving rise to the double pathway of distress-without-solution (fear, rage, and despair) and the false solution (such as amnesia, identification with the aggressive parent, or projection of the child's unbearable anger onto another).

If the child's experience of the parent is predominantly and traumatically negative, a large split-off pathway will result. Subsequently, stimuli that are related to the past threat will evoke the double pathway and the person will respond to perceived threats with split-off feelings of distress and false solutions that become habit patterns.

An individual's feelings develop as partial solutions to stimuli. *Identification*, achieved by combining the memory pathway of another's feelings, thoughts, or behavior with the pathway of the self's identity, occurs when it offers the best solution for a given stimulus.

Identification with a parent's loving, caring qualities may provide the best solution when an individual is distressed by the discomfort of another. Responding to the other's need will restore his comfort. For example, a little boy would become distressed when his baby sister cried. He would solve his, and her, distress by making funny faces for her until she stopped crying and began laughing. Caring and giving will also serve as solutions for the disequilibration that occurs when an individual's loving feelings for another are overstimulating.

Identification with a parent's aggression may provide the best solution for stimuli conveying danger. If such identification leads to an unrealistic sense of superiority over an aggressor, however, it is a false solution. Individuals with dissociative identity disorder often develop aggressive alters who erroneously feel that they can prevail over their abusers. Some people, in identifying with an aggressor, abuse others in response to stimuli that are related to abuse that they have experienced. When such a person perceives another as weak or vulnerable, it will remind him of his own past or ongoing vulnerability. His distress can be lessened by abusing the weaker one, by criticizing, teasing, bullying, or attacking.

WINNICOTT

D. W. Winnicott, a pediatrician who became a psychoanalyst, felt that if an infant had a "good-enough" mother he would develop healthily but that if his mother were out of tune with him, unempathic, he would experience her actions as noxious intrusions. The "good-enough" mother provides an adequate *holding environment*, that is, an understanding of her infant's needs. Without this, the infant develops a *false self*, a personality that conforms to his mother's expectations but that remains unaware of his own needs.

In the treatment of such an individual, as the therapist understands the patient's needs, the *true self* emerges. On occasions when the therapist fails to understand the patient, the lapses in empathy are experienced by the patient as were the noxious intrusions originally inflicted by his mother, causing him to respond with his false self or with anger. The therapist and patient work together to understand the significance of the empathic failures and come to understand the nature of the distress that the patient had experienced in his early life. This understanding allows the true self to prevail.

The new theory explains the false self as a false solution to an unbearable degree of distress caused by a parent's failures in providing for a child's needs. What would cause a parent to be so out of tune with a child? If the parent suffers from intense, chronic problems, they will monopolize awareness. For instance, a mother who is chronically distressed by having been neglected as a child may seek love from others, including her own child. Because the discomfort caused by her distress is greater than that caused by her child's, she will tend to her own needs rather than to his. The child's false solution includes an unawareness of the true self with its unsatisfied needs, and an attempt to comply with the parent's expectations in hopes of pleasing and getting something from the parent. Compliance can take many forms, from gentle attentiveness toward a needy mother to imitative ruggedness to satisfy a macho father.

The therapist, by providing understanding, serves as a new type of stimulus; one that evokes the true self, the repository of the patient's genuine needs and feelings. The therapist's misunderstandings, when they occur, serve as stimuli that are related to the parent's errors and therefore re-evoke the response of the false self. Because the therapist provides, at such moments, a complex stimulus, an interpretation will provide a true solution if the therapist recognizes and speaks to the split-off part, the true self. The patient's new awareness of his true self and his ability, therefore, to satisfy his genuine needs, provide a true solution for the distress.

SELF PSYCHOLOGY

While Freud focused on drives, and Klein and Winnicott on object relations, Heinz Kohut introduced a theory of the development of the self, a theory that has come to be called self psychology. According to Kohut, the infant responds to the imperfections of maternal care by attempting to preserve a state of perfection, both by developing a grandiose sense of himself, and by assigning his own sense of perfection to the parental figure, who becomes idealized and is viewed as omnipotent. The mother's delight in her child, expressed by the "gleam in her eye," provides *mirroring* of the child's grandiose sense of self. These figures, the *mirroring object* and the *idealized object*, are viewed as *selfobjects* because they are used to sustain the child's sense of perfection rather than as objects of his sexual and aggressive drives. In the normal course of events, as more is expected of the growing child, the parental mirroring becomes modified and the child experiences episodes of *optimal frustration* of the wishes for mirroring. The *grandiose self* is diminished and integrated into the personality as a healthy sense of self-esteem. The child also perceives imperfections in the parental figures, who thereby appear less exalted but still admirable. The child introjects the admirable qualities as his ideals.

If the child experiences traumatic lapses in his selfobject's mirroring (for example, if his mother is depressed and unable to appreciate him), he will be unable to modulate his grandiosity. It will remain a split-off part and he will need to find and use mirroring selfobjects, such as admiring friends, indefinitely. If he experiences traumatic disappointments in his idealized selfobject (for instance, if he learns that a parent has a serious flaw), he will be unable to introject it and will seek other selfobjects, such as esteemed mentors, to idealize.

In treatment, the individual develops a transference-like relationship to the therapist in which the therapist comes to be experienced as the mirroring and/or idealizing selfobject. When the patient experiences the therapist as either failing to mirror him or exhibiting an imperfection, the resulting distress at the momentary loss of the needed selfobject can be used to elucidate the experience of the past. It also provides an opportunity for optimal frustration of the need, which results in the attenuation of the grandiose self and/or the idealized object such that they can be integrated as healthy components of the personality.

The new theory proposes that the infant's sense of self-esteem is his cognitive and emotional response to the positive stimuli of his parent's love for and delight in him. As the individual develops, self-esteem results from his own appreciation of his attributes and accomplishments as well. When a parent becomes angry with or disappointed in him, the child's mind matches these negative stimuli with partial or false solutions. A partial solution may consist of feelings of depression, depletion, and worthlessness. False solutions in response to intense parental criticism or disappointment may include depersonalization, denial, and the formation of an illusory sense of self-esteem; but the unbearable feelings of low self-esteem and despair persist in the other branch of the double pathway. An illusory sense of self-esteem, if it continues, will intensify, developing into a feeling of superiority.

The individual will strive to find someone who appreciates

him, who will provide a new stimulus to which he can respond with a sense of feeling worthy. But admiration by a new person also reinforces the false feeling of superiority, which is still necessary because the split-off pathway of distress in response to the original traumas still exists. If the individual loses this supportive figure, he will respond as he did originally, with a variety of false solutions and the acquisition of a new source of support.

In normal development, the parents provide examples of solutions for problems. The child matches his distressing stimuli with memories of the parents' solutions. His parents' ideals, if they are useful, are also matched and thereby become the child's ideals as well. Feelings of admiration and awe are partial solutions for the overstimulation the child experiences as he perceives his parents' superiority. If a child experiences a traumatic disillusionment in a parent, that distress, if sufficiently intense, will be matched with a false solution: denial of the disillusionment, and either the continued veneration of the parent or the choice of another figure to look up to. A new person will, in addition to providing a substitute model, serve to reinforce the false solution of denial.

The individual will require such a figure indefinitely, to avoid the distress caused by the traumatic disillusionment still experienced in the other branch of the double pathway. As with the admiring figure described above, loss of a substitute model figure will cause an intense disequilibration to which the individual will respond by finding a new substitute model.

In the treatment of individuals with selfobject pathology, the therapist serves as a new figure. He provides support because he is attentive and non-judgmental and he serves as a model because of his emotional comfort and expertise. These qualities evoke healthy responses in the patient: feelings of self-worth and aspirations toward worthwhile ideals. They also reinforce the individual's false solutions. There will be moments at which the therapist fails to fulfill these roles (for instance, a lapse in attentiveness or display of a minor fault).

Because these failures are related to the failures of the parent, the therapist at this moment will constitute a complex stimulus: real figure and transference-like figure. A true solution will be provided when the therapist supplies the individual with an explanation of the current distress in relation to his past, addressing it to the split-off part of the double pathway.

INTERSUBJECTIVITY

In recent years, as therapists have studied the nature of the relationship between patient and therapist, many have come to view it as highly interactive; that is, not only does the patient respond to the therapist with transferences, projections, and defenses, but the therapist responds to the patient in these ways as well. In this view, the therapeutic process is therefore influenced by the conscious and unconscious participation of both parties as opposed to the previous view of the therapist as a neutral figure. This mutual participation and interaction has been called *intersubjectivity*. As these responses develop they lead to *enactments* in which each participant's feelings toward the other are expressed in behavior, largely unconsciously and often very subtly.

For example, Ms. Allen, an upper middle-class woman, had been raised in a male chauvinistic environment in which her brothers were favored. She was aware of her anger about this but not of her continuing feeling of inferiority and her tendency to defensively assume an air of superiority toward men. She related to her therapist, Dr. Brown, in this way, but so subtly that he did not initially pick up on it. On several occasions, however, he responded to her with a male chauvinistic remark, for which she indignantly berated him. After several of these episodes, Dr. Brown thought about his behavior and realized that he wanted to attack her because of her attitude. He had been raised by poor immigrants and had struggled to become assimilated into the upper middle-class culture of his profession. Yet, he now realized, he was still afraid that he might be seen as inferior. He was able to use this realization for both Ms. Allen's and his own benefit. When one or both participants become aware of their enactments, the origins can be explored and understood, furthering the therapeutic work. Although the goal in this work is, of course, to aid the patient, the therapist may also benefit from this new knowledge.

A therapist who develops an Inner Guide through self-hypnosis will benefit not only from the Inner Guide's superior memory and problem-solving ability, but also from its exceptional sensitivity to subliminal perceptions. The therapist's ability to detect subtle enactments will therefore be greatly enhanced. Moreover, a patient who develops an Inner Guide will find the therapy facilitated by its capabilities. It would behoove all therapists and patients to develop their Inner Guides.

GLOSSARY

automatic writing. A means of communication by which an Inner Guide supplies information by writing or typing.

complex stimulus. A stimulus that signifies two contradictory meanings, momentarily immobilizing the mind's ability to choose a response.

Davis Technique for Attaining Emotional Comfort. Self-hypnosis with the specific aim of developing an Inner Guide.

depersonalization. A state in which a person feels detached from himself, as though he is observing himself as he would another.

disequilibration. A disturbance that alters the stimulus level.

dissociation. A mental split that occurs when a false solution for a disequilibration is chosen, causing the formation of a double pathway. One branch contains the false solution and the other contains the continuing disturbance.

ego-dystonic. A maladaptive response that causes noticeable discomfort.

ego-syntonic. A maladaptive response that has become so in-grained as to be unnoticed.

false solution. An untrue solution chosen by the mind for a problem for which there are no (or inadequate) true or partial solutions. It does not diminish the disturbance but provides an alternative to experiencing it.

finger signals. A means of communication by which an

Inner Guide can cause specific fingers to be raised that signify "yes," "no," or "I don't know," in response to questions that are asked of it.

flashback. Aspects of a split-off mental pathway that slip into awareness when the disequilibration caused by maintaining the split is greater than the disturbance caused by ending it.

habit pattern. A response to a stimulus that becomes habitual because it solves the problem created by the stimulus.

identification. The result of combining the memory track of another person's behavior or feeling with the memory track of the self's identity.

Inner Guide. The mental pathway consisting of all past experiences of regained comfort, a sense of its own identity, and a wish to be helpful.

inner thought. A means of communication by which an Inner Guide expresses its thoughts in one's mind.

integration. The formation of a new mental pathway as a result of the simultaneous presence of a stimulus anda new solution for it, along with a related complex stimulus that facilitates the matching of the new solution to theproblem.

optimal stimulus level. The level of stimulation that provides maximum comfort.

partial solution. A solution that diminishes, but does not end, a disequilibration.

self-hypnosis. A mental state in which, with sufficient diminution of other stimuli, the desire to create a new wished-for state or entity in the mind becomes the strongest remaining stimulus, evoking the formation of that wished-for state or entity.

speedreading. Glancing at a page for just a moment so that the content will be registered in the memory for the Inner Guide's use.

stimulus. Any change. External stimuli consist of perceptions. Internal stimuli comprise thoughts, feelings, and mental images.

subliminal. Below the level of awareness.

transference. The tendency to expect from new external figures that which has been experienced from past figures due to their associative links.

true solution. A solution that completely ends a disequilibration.

BIBLIOGRAPHY

Bourne, L.E., and N.F. Russo. *Psychology: Behavior in Context*. New York: Norton, 1998.

Chmelar, R.D., and S. S. Fitt. *Diet for Dancers*. Pennington, N.J.: Princeton Book Company, 1990.

Davis, J.M. "A New Theory of Mental Functioning." Paper presented at the Wednesday Research Meeting of the Chicago Institute for Psychoanalysis, Chicago, Ill., March 22, 2000.

——. "A New Technique for Attaining Emotional Comfort." Paper presented at the Wednesday Research Meeting of the Chicago Institute for Psychoanalysis, Chicago, Ill., March 29, 2000.

Freud, S. *The Standard Edition of the Complete Psychological Works of Sigmund Freud*. London: The Hogarth Press, 1974.

Hammond, D.C. "Manual for Self-Hypnosis." Des Plaines, Ill.: American Society of Clinical Hypnosis, 1992.

Hebb, D.O. *The Organization of Behavior*. New York: Wiley, 1949.

Kleitman, N. *Sleep and Wakefulness*. Chicago: University of Chicago Press, 1963.

Kohut, H. *The Analysis of the Self*. New York: International Universities Press, 1971.

Lawrence, M. *In A World of their Own*. Westport, Conn: Praeger, 1997.

Levine, H.B., and R.J. Friedman. "Intersubjectivity and Interaction in the Analytic Relationship: A Mainstream View." *Psychoanal. Quart. 69*: 63-92, 2000.

Palombo, S. R. "Connectivity and Condensation in Dreaming." *J. Amer. Psychoanal. Assn. 40*: 1139-1159, 1992.

Pavlov, I.P. *Conditioned Reflexes.* New York: Dover, 1960. This book is a reproduction of Pavlov's original publication of 1927.

Pribram, K.H. *Languages of the Brain.* Englewood Cliffs, N.J.: Prentice-Hall, 1971.

Putnam, F.W. *Diagnosis and Treatment of Multiple Personality Disorder.* New York: Guilford Press, 1989.

Segal, H. *Introduction to the Work of Melanie Klein, Second Edition.* New York: Basic Books, 1964.

Siler, Brooke. *The Pilates Body.* New York: Broadway Books, 2000.

Solomon, P., H. Leiderman, J. Mendelson, and D. Wexler. "Sensory Deprivation." *Amer. J. Psychiat. 114*: 357-363, 1957.

Winnicott, D. W. *Through Paediatrics to Psycho-Analysis.* New York: Basic Books, 1975.

INDEX

Printed in the United States
22623LVS00001B/403-411